Marry with TASTE

TREASA BROGAN

TORC

For my husband, Pat, who showed me that marriage is a bed of roses and where to put the apostrophe!

First published in 1994 by
Torc
A division of Poolbeg Enterprises Ltd,
Knocksedan House,
123 Baldoyle Industrial Estate,
Dublin 13, Ireland

© Treasa Brogan 1994

The moral right of the author has been asserted.

A catalogue record for this book is available from the British Library.

ISBN 1 898142 03 3

All rights reserved. No part of this publication may be reproduced or transmitted in any form or by any means, electronic or mechanical, including photography, recording, or any information storage or retrieval system, without permission in writing from the publisher. The book is sold subject to the condition that it shall not, by way of trade or otherwise, be lent, resold or otherwise circulated without the publisher's prior consent in any form of binding or cover other than that in which it is published and without a similar condition, including this condition, being imposed on the subsequent purchaser.

Cover illustration by Cathy Dineen
Cover design by Poolbeg Group Services Ltd
Set by Poolbeg Group Services Ltd in Garamond 10.5/12
Printed by The Guernsey Press Ltd,
Vale, Guernsey, Channel Islands.

Let me not to the marriage of true minds
Admit impediments. Love is not love
Which alters when it alteration finds,
Or bends with the remover to remove.
O, no! it is an ever-fixed mark,
That looks on tempests and is never shaken;
It is the star to every wand'ring bark,
Whose worth's unknown, although his height be taken.
Love's not Time's fool, though rosy lips and cheeks,
Within his bending sickle's compass come;
Love alters not with his brief hours and weeks,
But bears it out even to the edge of doom.
    If this be error, and upon me prov'd
    I never writ, nor no man ever lov'd.

William Shakespeare

CONTENTS

INTRODUCTION	1
MARRIAGE THROUGH THE AGES	3
YOU ARE NOT ALLOWED TO MARRY	14
PROPOSE, ENGAGE, ANNOUNCE IT	15
MARRY IN MAY...CHOOSE THE DAY	21
THE GUEST LIST/THE GIFT LIST	26
DRESSING THE BRIDE	33
ACCESSORIES	45
DRESSING THE GROOM... FROM TOPPER TO TOE	52
HOW YOU CAN SAY IT WITH...FLOWERS	59
THE WEDDING CAKE	67
THE TRANSPORTATION	75
MAKING MUSIC	80
BUYING THE PHOTOGRAPHY	89
THE VIDEO	97
THE RECEPTION	102

MARRY ON A BUDGET	109
TOASTS, TALKS AND THANK YOUS	125
GETTING MARRIED IN A CATHOLIC CHURCH	132
MARRYING IN GALWAY CATHEDRAL	139
MARRYING IN THE PRO-CATHEDRAL	140
THE CHURCH OF IRELAND	142
MARRYING IN A METHODIST CHURCH	144
MARRYING IN THE REGISTRY OFFICE	147
MARRYING OUTSIDE THE PARISH	150
WHO PAYS FOR WHAT	156
DUTIFUL ATTENDANTS	158
THE HONEYMOON	162
AND SO TO WED... Adrian and Jackie Shine Damien O'Leary and Heather O'Hare Deirdre O'Kane and Stephen O'Connor Ann and Luke Hayden Gary and Frances Buchanan	166
THE SECOND MARRIAGE OR REMARRIAGE	191
COUNTDOWN TO WEDDING DAY	197

INTRODUCTION

So, someone has looked into someone else's eyes, and, somehow or other, what the poet, TS Eliot, described in another situation as, the overwhelming question, got asked. The answer was in the affirmative and now, as the song says, "we're goin' to the chapel (and/or the registry office) and we're goin' to get married."

Let there be no doubt about one thing, to make the leap from that simple, romantic moment when two people decide to wed to THE DAY when the wedding takes place is probably the most quantum leap each partner will ever make, in emotional and especially in sheer organisational terms.

Even before the first whisper of the wedding goes abroad, what you need most is a plan, because whether you intend to elope, have a civil or religious rite, or go for the full traditional ceremonial celebration, the better the plan the better chance you have for the wedding wheels to turn smoothly so that the bride and groom can actually enjoy and not just endure, the day.

Once the decision to marry has been made, the way and the day should be decided on, even before permission has been sought or granted or before the engagement ring is bought.

If no decision is made in advance of the romantic announcement, then the snowball effect occurs. It happens so rapidly, the happy pair can be left twirling helplessly in the whirlwind of other people's romantic notions, utterly dismayed to find that the romantic moment of the proposal had hardly been savoured, before the contentious how, where and when conversations had begun.

Hot Tip: If a couple decide together and in advance, exactly what sort of wedding they want, whether it's to be a mega or a muted affair, then, united in their determination, they have some chance of convincing their, albeit loving and well-intentioned, respective parents and relatives.

The perfect wedding, the wedding with taste, is a triumph of organisation over the trauma of what TS Eliot described as "decisions and revisions which a minute will reverse."

This book hopes to prepare the way of the wedding by provoking ideas, providing answers and presenting a set of checklists that will be a record of all decisions/contracts.

Get into the habit of writing everything down. As the hectic pace hots up good ideas, like soap bubbles, float away unless firmly anchored.

Enter the contact names, the company address and the outcome of every conversation, either as it occurs or immediately after it ends.

When you think of it, in the hatched, matched and despatched triangle of life, only the matched department can be planned to split-second timing. Doing the right thing, or more to the point, not wanting to be caught doing the wrong thing, often scares people into doing nothing.

It's amazing how riveted people are by the need to follow etiquette and convention. A good plan prevents paranoia and/or problems.

Next what you need is a box, a safe or a going-away suitcase, taken down from the top of the wardrobe, dusted and entitled "Operation Wedding Day." Into this receptacle will go all of the pre-nuptial paraphernalia you are likely to gather between this and your wedding day.

MARRIAGE THROUGH THE AGES

Today's marriages almost all conform to a conventional pattern of courtship, engagement, religious or civil marriage ceremony, followed by a celebratory knees-up.

The limits and determinants of the celebration tend to be set by taste and money. How will the rituals and conventions of marriage be viewed in a century's time? If one is to judge from the plethora of images and snapshots of marriages throughout history, they will be used as a mirror to reflect on the shortcomings, prejudices and idiosyncrasies of our time. Will the marriage of a couple in a hot air balloon be seen as desertion or devilment? What about the couple who did a bungee jump immediately after taking their vows—what layers of symbolism will be attached to the inspiring leap into the unknown?

Patterns have evolved that emphasise the male dominance within the rituals of the wedding. The father or a male relative escorts the bride to the church, he makes a speech at the banquet, as does the priest, the bride and her mother were never asked to speak at the wedding table, although many of today's brides are having their say.

It is likely that the increasing political and social freedoms which women enjoy have greatly, and for the better, affected the institution of marriage. New values of society have led to an increase in separations of married couples, whether legally sanctioned or just pragmatic. The transition from old to new values will influence the institution of marriage with an increase in the number of second marriages or relationships.

Marriage is formed through a vow or an agreement. Society mobilises its forces to cement permanent unions. From the most primitive to the most developed society, it is solemnised and contracted at a hallowed and specially appropriate place, in churches or temples, in the public place or a village, or before the gods of the domestic hearth. Not only have the couple to exchange gifts and vows, but the community is drawn in. Marriage is a public proclamation, an announcement of a commitment. It established a domestic unit which in most societies provides an environment for child-rearing. The story of marriage throughout the ages is rich, full of interest and significance. It holds a mirror to many societies. It is social history with a tincture of sex. Many features have conditioned the attitude of society towards marriage. The needs of children, the economic and associated family pressures, the regulations and traditions which have evolved from a married person—the list could go on and on. In Irish society, the most obvious influence on marriage has been the Christian ideal of marriage as a life-long exclusive commitment.

What constitutes a legal marriage? No single answer would cover the multiplicities of civil and religious regulations as they evolved through the centuries. The strict rules stipulating that a marriage might be only dissolved by the death of a spouse were not echoed in earlier periods of history.

Early Roman law forbade soldiers to marry and soldiering rendered a previous marriage invalid—echoes here of the rural distaste for the tradition of army enlistment "gone for a soldier."

The Celtic code of laws, the Brehon Laws, gave flexibility to either marriage partner to dissolve the union. Divorce and remarriage were allowed. A woman could divorce her husband if he was sterile, a gossip about the marriage bed, a wife beater, a homosexual, or if he failed to provide maintenance.

The man could divorce his wife for abortion,

infanticide, infertility or bad management of the home. Divorce by mutual consent was also possible. Going abroad on a pilgrimage was considered adequate grounds for ending a marriage. The Irish historian, Ken Nicholls, contends that the older Celtic pattern lasted to the end of the seventeenth century, with "Christian matrimony" being a rare exception. Women could hold property in their own right, and this was removed by the plantation schemes of the seventeenth century.

Up to the eleventh century, casual polygamy appears to have been general with divorce easy to obtain. In the early Middle Ages, all that marriage meant for most people seems to have been a private contract between two families involving property exchange. For those without property, it was a private contract between two individuals, enforced by the community sense of what was right. A church ceremony was unnecessary and expensive, especially since divorce by mutual consent was a widely accepted practice. The religious ideal of monogamous, indissoluble marriage was not universally accepted. Before 1754 in the UK, there were many ways of contracting a marriage.

For those with property, it involved a number of steps. The first was a written contract between the parents about property rights, the second involved the "spousals," or contract of marriage by the couple. According to ecclesiastical law, the spousals were as legally binding as the church wedding.

Any sort of exchange of promises in the presence of witnesses which was followed by cohabitation was regarded in law as a valid marriage. Only after the Reformation did the Catholic Church require the presence of a priest to make a marriage valid and binding.

While the church ceremony gained in importance in the Anglican church, its lawyers continued to recognise the spousals before witness as binding. A spousal followed by consummation could not be legally broken at a later date, it was binding for life. As this eighteenth century writer shows, it was widely held that in the eighteenth century, sexual cohabitation was practised after the betrothal:

"Contracted persons are in a middle degree betwixt single persons and married persons: they are neither simply single, nor actually married. Many take liberty after a contract to know their spouse, as if they were married: an unwarrantable and dishonest practise."

One English historian has written that one-third of the brides of the eighteenth and nineteenth centuries were pregnant when they married.

A spousal where the couple exchanged exact actual marriage vows was regarded in ecclesiastical law as irrevocable.

The regulations of marriage were changed in Ireland after the Reformation, initiated by Henry VIII (Behan's rude rhyme of the Church of Ireland being built on the bollox of Henry VIII is an interesting commentary of the sexual imperatives of marriage).

Church weddings these days are solemnised inside the church building but this did not always hold. Chaucer's Wife of Bath took five husbands, all at the church door. The various elements of the liturgies of marriage—legal preliminaries, the giving away of the bride, the formal grant of dowry by the bridegroom, the exchange of promises, the blessing of the ring, and its placing on the third finger of the left hand, followed by nuptial mass—evolved in the eleventh and twelfth centuries. Once the wedding ceremony at the door was finished, then the couple entered the church to be blessed by the priest, "in the presence of the church." It was the constant aim of the church from the twelfth to the sixteenth century to bring the wedding service into the church building. The definition of marriage adopted by Pope Alexander III in 1160 and preserved as the basic minimum for a valid marriage until the Council of Trent—in the Church of England until the eighteenth century—involved consent before witnesses so a marriage could be made binding, without being "in the presence of the church."

It was common in some parts of Europe to exchange marriage vows away from the church. In England, this private contract was made clandestinely and without intention of resorting to the church. Marriages could be contracted and were under the ash tree, in a bed, in a garden, in a field, in a blacksmith's shop, at a tavern. It was evident that a church ceremony was not an essential feature of matchmaking.

The Catholic Church's response, through the reforms of the Council of Trent, was to state that a marriage had to be validly sworn in the presence of a priest and two witnesses.

The prior publication of banns lessened significantly the possibility of secret marriages, as did the registration of marriages in church records. Until 1563, couples did not have to be married in a church for the union to be recognised by the Catholic Church. The couple's consent was more important than church consent. Church formalities would thereafter have to be followed.

Such definite guidelines did not apply in English Protestant churches until 1753, when church ceremonies became legally binding, so that a prior oral contract would no longer be a reason for annulling a later marriage in church.

Enforcement of the law was transferred to the civil court from ecclesiastical institutions. The primacy of the church wedding was established, after which the civil register was signed. Public registration was necessary to stem the possibility of bigamy and secret marriages. Divorce now became less a possibility, with couples opting for a separation of bed and board, accompanied by a marriage settlement. Neither party could remarry in the event of a split. The road to nullity was fenced off with strict definitions, away from the medieval impediments which could lead to a church dissolution. After the Reformation, an annulment in England could be obtained for male impotence, a pre-contract, or consanguinity. Marriage became an institution dissolved only by death.

The lower orders in England were less respectful of such restriction. It was easy to run away and never to be heard from again. "Wife-sale," whereby a woman was led to the market with a halter around her neck, sold on to the highest bidder, and led away by halter, was an economic ritual freeing the husband from future responsibility for his wife. It had a medieval origin, the last recorded case being 1887. Thomas Hardy drew on it in one of his novels, showing how fresh it remained in folk memory.

Recently a Dublin vet and his bride placed two heifer-figures on their wedding cake. This has echoes of the social and sordidly economic criteria used to match marriage partners in previous centuries. How this has changed from the facts of partnership of 200 years ago.

The modern ideal of marriage is based on the primacy of adult love. Dowry and income are not laid in the scales, and conform to the historical model of the marriage which evolved in recent centuries—the "companionate marriage."

What was it?

"Men should maintain their wives as becomes partners: they (the wives) are friends and companions to their husbands, not slaves, nor menial servants; they are the inseparable companions in misery and misfortune." (*New Duty of Man*, pub, eighteenth century)

Sir Thomas Overbury, in 1614, described a good wife as, "more than a friend, an equal with him in the

Marry with Taste

yoke. He without her is (but) half himself."

Many declarations of this ideal can be found in English poetry, drama and letters before the eighteenth century. But it was an ideal wed in practice to an economic yoke. In Victorian times, novels of many volumes were churned out and the usual theme of the romantic novel was the triumph of love over lucre. This sentiment marked a bold change in the general attitude towards marriage, one which has persisted to the present day. The companionate marriage was a step towards the nuclear family. The family unit now rose or fell on its own resources.

Family members lost contact with the wider kin, especially the aged. Some continental observer noted, in 1828, that grown-up children and parents had become almost strangers, with domestic life as a label applying only to husband, wife and dependent children.

In 1838, Charles Darwin was contemplating marriage. He wrote his reservations and expectations, balancing in the scales the benefits and drawbacks of marriage. In pencil on a blue sheet, he drew up his cost-benefit analysis:

"This is the question
Marry/Not Marry"

Under "Marry," he jotted down the element of comforts:
"Children, if it please God. Constant companion who will feel interested in one, a friend of old age, object to be loved and played with, better than a dog anyhow.
Home and someone to take care of house, classics of music and female chit-chat. These things good for one's health.
Forced to visit and receive relation—terrible loss of time.
My God, it is unthinkable to think of spending one's whole life, like a neuter bee, working,

working, and nothing after all. No, no, won't do. Imagine living all one's days solitarily in smoky, dirty London House, only picture to yourself a nice soft wife, on a sofa, with a good fire, and books and music perhaps, compare this vision with dingy reality of Great Marlborough Street.

Marry, Marry, Marry, QED"

On the opposite scale he simply wrote the contrasting elements. No children, for example. He then listed the advantages of not marrying and remaining a bachelor:
"Freedom to go where one liked—choice of society and little of it. Conversation of clever men at clubs. Not forced to visit relatives and to bend in every trifle.
Not to have the expense and anxiety of children, perhaps quarrelling. Loss of time—cannot read in the evenings. Fatness and idleness.
Anxiety and responsibility, less money for books etc.
If many children, forced to gain one's bread. But then it is very bad for one's health to work too much. Perhaps my wife won't like London, then the sentence and degradation with indolent idle fool."

Having considered both sides of the argument he married Emma Wedgwood on 29th January 1839, just before his thirtieth birthday.

Later on that year he developed his theory of evolution of how species evolved through natural selection. How ironic that he should have selected his own life partner that year.

The (generally) low key, indoor celebrations after the modern wedding ceremony contrast with the boisterous day of the rabblement, using the excuse of a wedding to promote civil excitement. Take the match between an elderly man and a younger woman, often unpopular because it threatened to disencfranchise the children of a first marriage. Such marriages prompted ribald public demonstrations, as recalled by Kevin Dannaher.

He served in the Irish army in the 1940s at the Glen of Imail, in County Wicklow. One night, he heard a great burst of sound, booing, catcalls, and the banging of metal and horn blowing. The guard was turned out, until a local man in the camp explained that because a farmer with a grown family had just married a young girl, the local young men staged this loud demonstration outside his house, and the tradition was known locally as "horning old Johnny."

This custom of "horning" was common in Leinster and east Ulster. Patrick Kavanagh refers to the custom in Monaghan,

"Old buckets rusty holed, with half hung handles,
were drums to play when old men married wives."

French and English examples of this carnival can also be found.

Marriage patterns are heavily determined by social and economic conditions. The famine years in Ireland constitute a watershed. The stream of emigration for the next century led to rigid constraints on marriage. The majority of each generation left. In the post-famine years, men in Meath were usually three or four times more likely than Mayomen *not* to have found a wife by age of fifty. But by the 1950s, a majority of Connachtmen in rural areas were single. For rural men, marriage time was decided by the timing of succession to land or economic independence. Women had better prospects, as their marriages did not depend on economic dowry.

Christian marriage in Ireland, as elsewhere, is bound up with parenthood and the rearing of children. This traditional unit is not seen in contemporary Ireland as the sole mechanism for parenting. The changing pattern can be seen in the increasing number of women availing of "unmarried mother" allowance, and the number of single mothers retaining their children. In 1976, unmarried mothers accounted for 3.7% of births, while the figure for 1990 was 14.5%. The increase in non-martial fecundity has happened at a time of falling births. Some Irish population analysts expressed concern when the national fecundity rate fell 2.11%, below the point where a population remain stable. In, 1989, nearly 17,000 nearly unmarried mother 5 claimed the relevant allowance, compared with 3.334 in 1976.

This change in status of the family unit has not been fully recognised. The family in Ireland was placed in a legal closet in the 1937 Constitution, with the state pledging to "guard with special care the institution of marriage, on which the family is founded and to protect it against attack." The term "family," according to Claire Carney, was not actually defined until the Supreme Court in 1966 determined that the family referred to in the constitution was "the family which is founded upon the institution of marriage." The abolition of the concept of illegitimacy in 1987, the extention of the notion of family in tax legislation, the ongoing political debate on the possibility of divorce in the Republic of Ireland—all point to the practical irrelevance of the 1937 notion of a family, as based on the family unit as legalised through marriage under the law of the state.

As has happened down the ages and as is happening even as this book is being written, the rules of marriage are once again undergoing legal changes.

In 1993, the Minister for Equality and Law Reform, Mervyn Taylor, introduced a bill to raise the age of mariage to eighteen years. He said, "It is generally accepted that the current age of sixteen is too young. This provision is designed to protect the institution of marriage and to indicate the seriousness of the contract which couples enter into on marriage."

Currently there are many sociological studies taking

place to establish exactly where the 1990s marriage is at.

With one-in-four unmarried mothers living with the father of their child and fifty per cent of unmarried fathers supporting their child's development, the evidence suggests that we are entering The Paperless Era of Marriage.

In *Marriage in Ireland*, Donnchadh O'Corrain refers to a controversy amongst early Irish lawyers (about AD 700) as to whether monogamy or polygamy was the more proper.

One clerical lawyer solved the problem by reference to the Old Testament. "If the chosen of God, David, Solomon and Jacob, lived in polygamy, is it not more difficult to condemn it, than to praise it?"

Proof if there need be, that marriage is indeed, gone back to the future!

The following books were consulted for research on the history of marriage:

Marriage in Ireland, ed. Art Cosgrove (Dublin, 1985)
The Medieval Idea of Marriage, CNL Brooke (Oxford, 1989)
In and out of Marriage: Irish and European Experience. ed. G Kelly (Dublin, 1992)
The Family, Sex, and Marriage in England, 1500—1800, L Stone (London, 1977)
Marriage and Love in England, 1300—1840, A Macfarlane (London, 1986)

YOU ARE NOT ALLOWED TO MARRY

❦

Your natural mother, adoptive or former adoptive mother
    Mother's brother, sister, husband, mother or father
    Mother's mother's husband, mother's father's wife

Your father, adoptive or former adoptive father
    Father's brother, sister, wife, mother or father
    Father's mother's husband, father's father's wife

    The daughter, adoptive or former adoptive daughter
    Daughter's husband, son or daughter
    Daughter's daughter's husband, daughter's son's wife

Son, adoptive or former adoptive son
    Son's wife, son or daughter
    Son's daughter's husband or son's son's wife

Sister, sister's son or daughter
    Brother, brother's son or daughter

Wife's mother or daughter
    Wife's mother's mother, wife's father's mother
    Wife's son's daughter, wife's daughter's daughter

Husband's father or son
    Husband's father's father, husband's daughter's son

PROPOSE, ENGAGE, ANNOUNCE IT

"Nothing in the world is single;
All things, by a law divine,
In one spirit meet and mingle.
Why not I with thine?"
Love's Philosophy, PB Shelley.

The proposal, whether couched in poetic or paltry terms, can be made at the top of the Macgillycuddy Reeks, the bottom of a ravine, over a candlelit dinner, or under the swansdown duvet; the location and execution is only as limited as the imagination of the proposer.

Having decided on the sort of wedding day you would like, the very next step is to tell the respective parents. Tradition has it the bride's parents are told first. This dates back to the time when the would-be groom grovelled at the feet of his would-be father-in-law. While times have changed and that custom has almost if not entirely died off, seeking the approval of both sets of parents, before the formal announcement takes place, has to be a good way of giving the new in-law relationship a chance to get off on the right foot.

In the old days the woman's virtue was taken as read, while the character of the man was rigourously checked. Nowadays, both partners are considered equally responsible. In America, as well as character assessments, the norm for most couples is to swap health, wealth and Aids-free certificates before vowing anything. The old custom of presenting the engagement ring at the time of the proposal has long since waned. What with diamonds being a girl's best friend, most women want to pick their own.

Some couples prefer to buy the engagement ring before announcing the betrothal. It's entirely optional.

Nowadays, the engagement announcement is a fairly casual affair anyway, with the news spreading out by word of mouth, mainly on the telephone.

If you belong to a large family and would like, if possible, for each member to find out your good news at the same time, then it might be better to tell it by letter. Write a short note, postcard, or even a computer print-out, giving the details. Post the letters together and then stand by for a deluge of telephone calls.

Obviously, if you've landed a rich tycoon, a media star, an exotic princess or a knighted aristocrat you won't need to tell the world. Rather will it be knocking on your door for you to tell them. Witness the recent, global, headline-making saturation coverage of the engagement of U2's Adam Clayton to Naomi Campbell.

For the majority, however, a formal announcement, if desired, can be made in the parish gazette (usually for free), or in the local or national papers.

Engagement notices can be pompous, like:

Aishling Brown BA, MA, Ph. D. (Phil, OU)
Robert Black, MA Eng.
Bob and Brenda Black, the steel magnates from Ohio, announce the betrothal of their first born heir, Robert II, chief engineer of HDH to Aishling, daughter of Sean Brown, MD, of Brown Zinc Int. and Mary Brown (QS). Both families are pleased with this union of minds and metals.
Or plain...Miley, the small farmer from Glenroe, and Biddy, the mushroom grower from Arklow, are, together with their families, delighted to announce their engagement. Hooley details to follow.

The practice of announcing the actual date and time of the wedding stopped when it was discovered that the most ardent readers of the engagement columns were would-be burglars, who carefully filed away the details in their filofaxes, all the better to collect the presents while the family were elsewhere. Engagement notices also attract a lot of unasked for bumph mail.

The Wedding Rings

"Oh! How many torments lie,
in the small circle of a wedding ring!"
The Double Gallant, Colley Cibber, 1734.

According to the 1856 edition of *Enquire Within:*
"If a gentlemn want a wife, he wears a ring on the first finger of the left hand; if he is engaged, he wears it on the second finger; if he is married, on the third; and on the fourth if he never intends to be married. When a lady is not engaged (note the shift in emphasis) she wears a hoop or diamond on her first finger; if engaged on her second; if married on her third; and on the fourth if she intends to die a maid."

The tradition of wearing a ring on the third finger of the left hand to denote marriage dates back to an ancient belief that a vein ran straight from that finger to the heart.

The Princess of Wales, huge sapphire, nesting in a cluster of diamonds, set a trend that continues today, fifteen years later and even after the demise of her marriage to Prince Charles.

Old versus new? Lots of people set out to buy an antique engagement ring, myself included. But when I found I couldn't get the design I wanted, I opted for a new ring which my fiancé helped to design with the jewellery manufacturer, Mr David Blackman of J & Z Blackman, 34 Anne's Lane South, Dublin 2, Ph 6770201.

If you decide to buy an old ring, ensure the stones are secure and in good condition. Repairs can be expensive and remember, antique rings are often too fragile for everyday use.

At the Powerscourt Centre, off Grafton Street, I saw an antique wedding band for £85, three-stone engagement rings started at £200.

Get the Antique Valued, for Free, Before you Buy

A ring has to be one hundred years old before it is classified as an antique ring, although traders tend to use the term much more liberally. At the Howth Sunday Fair, I was offered an antique frog ring for £40. When I murmured knowledgeably that it was in marvellous condition for a ring dating back to 1893, the lady behind the stall immediately demurred, admitting no, it wasn't, strictly speaking, an antique ring, as it was only forty years old.

Perhaps the lady knew a little bit about the law. When buying an antique ring, the onus of antiquity lies with the vendor.

The Assay Office at Dublin Castle, Ph 4751286, offers a free jewellery education to anyone who wishes to avail of it. The office is open 8.30 am—3.45 pm, Monday to Friday. During those hours items are dated and valued, free of charge, no appointment necessary. I'm told that ninety-nine per cent of the queries are catered for on the spot. The remaining one per cent will be referred by the Assay Office to the Antique Plate Committee. They meet on a bi-monthly basis, depending on demand. Again, expert specialist advice is offered free of charge, under the auspices of the Assay Office.

Ergo, nobody has anybody but themselves to blame if they buy a dud antique. If a ring is hallmarked, it has a date letter. This date letter represents the year in which the ring was registered. If a ring isn't hallmarked, it probably came out of a barm brack or is made of brass. If in doubt, bring your antique item (and the vendor if necessary) to the Assay Office.

Rings are mainly a matter of colour and fashion. Many are bought for their calendar (the bride's birthstone) and character symbolism.

January	Garnet	*consistency and truth*
February	Amethyst	*genuine love*
March	Aquamarine	*courage*

Marry with Taste

April	Diamond	*purity/innocence*
May	Emerald	*contentment*
June	Pearl	*health/beauty*
July	Ruby	*devotion/deep love*
August	Peridot	*joy*
September	Sapphire	*wisdom*
October	Opal	*hope/inconstancy*
November	Topaz	*faithfulness/loyalty*
December	Turquoise	*success*

Gold is mixed with other metals, else it would not be pliable. The carat is the amount of pure gold per 24 parts. 22-carat gold is almost pure and very expensive but it's also more delicate and will wear away sooner than the more robust 18-carat. The word carat means weight for diamonds and purity for gold. White gold is 18-carat gold alloyed with silver. Platinum is the most enduring metal. It keeps its colour and polish. Even though most couples match the metals in the engagement and wedding rings, with use, the solid wedding band usually wears down the thin underside of the engagement ring.

It's very difficult to tell a good stone from a bad, unless you are a jeweller. You only have to visit the auction rooms to know the huge difference in value that takes place with stones of only the slightest difference in clarity, colour, size and shape.

When you set out to buy the ring, borrow or buy an eye-glass. If nothing else it will signal to the jeweller that you are a couple who know your onions, to coin a metaphor. If, when you look down the barrel of the eye-glass, you see black speckles, cloudiness, and/or a yellow tinge then the stone is less than perfect. If, on the other hand, you cannot see these things with the naked eye, the jeweller is a reliable trustworthy goldsmith and the price is right, go for it. Ask about the wedding ring when buying the engagement ring. For instance, if the engagement ring doesn't have a straight head you will probably need to get a ring specially made so that the two will fit snug as bugs when joined together on the big day, just like the bride and groom.

Engagement and Wedding Ring Checklist

- What design has been agreed:

- What stones:

- How many:

- What weight is the gold:

- Does the engagement ring require a matching wedding ring:

- How much for engagement ring. How much for wedding rings:

- When to collect the engagement ring:

- When to collect the wedding ring:

- How to clean both:

- How much to insure engagement ring for: (Often different to how much)

MARRY IN MAY...CHOOSE THE DAY

"This day I breathed first: time is come round,
And where I did begin, there shall I end;"
William Shakespeare

If there is one certainty about setting your wedding date, it is that no matter what time of year you choose you have an exact equal chance that the weather will be fine or freezing!

Two of my neighbours extended their gardens recently. This required tons of clay. One being impatient threw caution to the winds and ordered his mountain of earth in December. He got a bright sunny day and with help from the neighbours had it shovelled in within a matter of hours. The other planned a June delivery. He got torrential floods which washed away some of the clay and made the remainder desperately difficult to lift and shift.

I attended a wedding during that famous flooded June 1993. The morning was a winter's day, heavy rain, high winds and a shower of hailstones swirled around the church like elemental confetti. Inside the guests froze in their light summer attire. But by the time the ceremony was over, the wind had subsided, the rain ceased, the sun came out and everyone smiled.

The Month—Marry in May, Rue the Day!

The moral of these stories is, you cannot pick a good day, it all depends on the gods. However, if the weather is unpredictable in Ireland, it's reasonably dependable in other countries, so your honeymoon destination may be the determining factor in the season you choose.

When you have decided on the month, decide on a day before a date. If you intend marrying in a church you will also have to remember the church calendar. Many churches frown on, if they don't absolutely forbid, weddings during Lent, especially Holy Week, when, if the wedding is allowed, flowers and church decoration may be forbidden.

The "In" Season

Despite the unpredictability of our weather, most summer weddings are planned in the hope of a shimmering sunny day. June, July and August are the big months. But they are also the big holiday months so if you especially want your favourite aunt who is great crack and a certainty to keep the party going make sure you give her plenty of warning.

Before you announce the date, check the availability of the hotel, church, and anyone whose services you especially want—photographer/musician.

Ireland has the highest number of house owners in the EC. Many couples decide to wait until their house is in order before they marry.

If that's your choice, the buying of the house will obviously become a major part of your wedding preparations. But it needn't be a deciding factor on when you marry. If the house is not quite ready you can camp out, rent, or maybe stay with relatives if the interim period is short. It used to be that if the house was ready before the wedding, the groom moved in alone. Now, increasingly, the couple set up house first and marry later.

If your idea of nuptial nirvana is totally tied up with a summer wedding followed by a foreign sun-drenched holiday, then go for it.

Marry with Taste

The "Out" Seasons

If you are not a sun worshipper and plan to honeymoon in a city then there are numerous advantages to an autumn/spring or winter wedding.

1. Because you have decided to marry out of season, so to speak, you will not be expecting good weather but may very well be surprised to get a pet day.

2. Yours will probably be the only wedding reception on the day both in the church, and at the venue.

3. Bearing in mind the endless end-of-term celebrations that take place in summer, the florists and photographers will not be as stretched as they often are in summer. "There are no weddings, not one," said florist Merna O'Neill when I talked to her in November.

4. Guests are unlikely to be away on holidays.

5. Hotel out-of-season offers and extras are a real saving and bonus.

6. Ditto for travel companies.

The Day

Marry on a Monday for health, Tuesday wealth, Wednesday is the best day (the day of the royals), Thursday brings losses, Friday crosses, Saturday bad luck! You can see that the power of the superstition has given way to the power of economic and social constraints.

For most places of worship, Sunday is either simply not allowed or definitely discouraged. Sunday, being the busy day of the week for clergymen and clergywomen, it's easy to understand why. For Catholics some holy days are out too.

At the Registry Office, Saturday and Sunday are out. Monday is a bad day, from the point of view of flowers. Monday, Tuesday, Wednesday and Thursday are good from a monetary point of view because many of the wedding services give special mid-week rates.

But if the bride and groom save money by marrying mid-week, it can put financial pressure on the guests who have to sacrifice a day's pay.

Other guests may be unavailable mid-week simply due to work pressures. Or be unable to take a day off due to the holiday commitments of the company. Friday weddings are as expensive as Saturday weddings. They have all the mid-week disadvantages, although a Friday afternoon wedding means that only a half-day is required and the guests have the weekend to recover from the ravages if they have over-indulged on the celebrations. Saturday has been, by far and away, the most popular wedding day for yonks. Hotels are often engaged two years ahead! Don't doubt it. Book early.

The Time

In very olden times, the law decreed that marriages take place in the morning. And like many rules, the cultural tradition continued long after the law had been changed. If you are catching a plane or a train on the evening of your wedding, then obviously a morning wedding is a must.

In recent years the morning slot has given way to the new favoured, early afternoon. A number of factors have combined to make this an attractive option.

1. For mid-week marriages it has the advantage that guests need only take a half-day's leave.

2. The wedding ceremony, reception and arrival of evening visitors dovetails nicely to leave just the right amount of time for banqueting, banjoing and bacchanalia!

3. So many hotels include overnight accommodation to the bride and groom, with the price of the reception.

Marry with Taste

Get Thee to the Church on Time

I'll never forget a wedding I attended in Tubber Parish Church, Co Offaly. The month was April, the snow was on the ground, the church was about to close for roof repairs and the heating was on the blink.

The bride being thirty minutes late, (she'd had another cup of tea), only ensured that the icicles were firmly in place before the wedding ceremony began. Afterwards, when we thawed out, we had a brilliant traditional country hooley in the Grand Hotel in Moate, the best I've ever known. But the experience made me sympathise with a certain, Monsignor Patrick Leonard, parish priest of Swinford. He issued an ultimatum to the brides of Mayo that they will find him at home if they are not on time. After forty years and 1,000 wedding ceremonies, the Monsignor announced that he is "fed up with late-arriving brides." He gave warning that the next late bride would find him at home and that he would return at his own convenience. You have been warned.

THE GUEST LIST/THE GIFT LIST

❦

"The Wedding Guest here beat his breast,
For he heard the loud bassoon."
The Rime of the Ancient Mariner,
Samuel Taylor Coleridge

If you are very lucky, your wedding list may very well include a guest as well-travelled and as literate as the Ancient Mariner, hopefully he won't talk for quite as long!

There was a time when the guest list and the gift list ran on parallel lines. Now, like a train track, they've merged into one as the practice of the gift list being included with the formal wedding invitation gathers momentum.

Inviting the Guests

The current fashion of inviting one bevy of relatives and friends to the formal church and wedding breakfast and another lot to the informal evening/disco reception, means that you are in effect having two receptions and therefore must send out two separate invitations.

Who to Ask—The Seven Tribes of Israel

How to separate the sheep from the goats, that's the question. Of the many different arrangements that are needed to plan a wedding, undoubtedly the one with the most contentious potential is the compiling of the guest list. If they have not realized it before, knocking the guest list into shape should convince the couple that a wedding may take only two people but it often seems to include the seven tribes of Israel.

Should the rake be invited? If so, who will be the minder so that the respectability of the family can be preserved? That first cousin whose recent wedding was confined to her immediate family because she wisely spent her money on a house deposit, should she be invited just because all of the other cousins are included?

Blood is an excellent boundary line. You might decide to invite the brothers and sisters of both sets of parents and no cousins. If you adhere to it rigidly, no one can feel left out. You can't include one cousin/aunt/uncle because you like them or because they once gave you a loan of £500 or because he/she is the family celeb. Such selective inclusions only alienate the rest of the family and the resentment will send a chill through the celebrations.

The same applies to children. You cannot invite your favourite godchild and leave out all of the other nieces and nephews. And you must make it perfectly clear that children are not to be brought. I was at a wedding where a couple arrived with their only darling child in tow, smiling assurances that they would pay for the child's portion. But the other guests assumed that the child had been invited, and they began to wonder why their own little darlings had been slighted.

The list of exclusion clauses and causes is endless. Try to cover as may potential danger spots as possible.

Q: Who does the asking?
A: He/She who pays the piper.

There is one simple guiding principle, he/she who pays the piper calls the tune. As the bride's parents, usually (though not always) pay for the reception, they will decide on how many can be invited.

It's customary for the bride and groom, having obtained the groom's list of guests from the groom's parents, to collaborate with the bride's parents in order to work out the fine details. Whatever number of guests has been decided on is usually divided half and half between the family of the bride and the family of the groom.

Sending Out Invitations

Invitations can take many forms, from the formal to the novel, a phone-around, handwritten letters, cards, comic-strips, balloons, baubles, paper hats!

Though the centuries may have changed the mode of invitation, from the traditional hand-engraved in copperplate script to the computer print-out, the message is still essentially the same.

Chanel Wedding Stationery, 61 Chanel Rd, Artane, Dublin 5, Ph 8475823, is a wholly Irish-owned company.

Their advice is to order stationery at least three months before the wedding. The average cost for a matching, personalised set of day and evening invitations, Thank You Cards and Place Cards, is between £85 and £120.

When you decide on the number of guests it's a good idea to order extra invitations because re-ordering is more expensive than the initial cost and it's usually handy to have stand-by invitations in case, like the CAO places in universities, a number of your first round guests send regrets and you may decide to send out a second round of invites. This happens in June and July when so many people are off on holidays.

The writing of the names on the invitations is a job for the family calligrapher or, failing that, the neatest writer. Chanel supply special silver/gold pens so that the writing on the card and envelope matches the printed invitation.

It's usual to send one invitation to a couple or whole family. If only some members of one family are invited, make sure to use their full names—John Clarke Senior, so that no mix-ups occur say if John Clarke Junior opens the letter first.

The Gift List or How to Avoid the Seven ironing-boards Syndrome

> "Scatter these well meaning idioms,
> Into the smoky spring that fills,
> The suburbs, where they will be lost,
> There are no trophies of the sun."
> *Praise for an Urn,* Hart Crane, 1899-1932

Wedding presents have certainly, in the words of WB, "changed, changed utterly." Whatever happened to the picture of the Sacred Heart accompanied by a Child of Prague statue!

Where once guests used to wear their nerves and the soles of their shoes paper thin trying to find presentable pressies, now they can pick from a pre-selected gift list, something within their own price range, simply by picking up the phone. Very civil.

Marks and Spencer, 24/29 Mary Street, Dublin 1, Ph 8728833, are the first store in Dublin to compile a special wedding list brochure. It works like this:

About four months before the wedding, the couple choose a range of items they'd like from the wedding gift book. This list is held on the Marks and Spencer computer list in all of their stores, Ireland, England, Scotland and Wales. Marks and Spencer supply cards, about the size of a credit card, stating, "Our wedding list is at M & S."

These cards are sent out with the wedding invitation cards for the formal reception, not for the evening reception.

Once a gift has been chosen, it is taken off the computerised list obviously to prevent duplication. Immediately after the wedding M & S will send a final list to the bride and groom, showing the items purchased and the name of the purchaser, to facilitate the sending of thank you cards.

The wedding catalogue includes Marks and Spencer gift vouchers in denominations of £1, £5, £10 and £25. There's no charge for this wedding list service. Roches Stores don't keep a wedding list.

Switzers, Grafton Street, Dublin 2, Ph 6776821, do. After the wedding Switzers will send the couple a list of the items purchased but not a list of purchasers. So if you missed the little card in the box then you could end up not knowing who sent what and Great Aunt Bertha could get thanked for a voucher when she in fact sent a vacuum cleaner.

Arnotts, Henry Street, Dublin 1, Ph 8721111. Wedding list service is confined to keeping a wedding list compiled by the couple and gift wrapping the items. They don't compile either a list of the items purchased or by whom.

Clerys, O'Connell Street, Dublin 1, Ph 8786000, have been running a wedding list for some years now. They too supply the couple with the cards for the wedding invitations. Clerys find that most guests prefer to deliver the gift themselves but Clerys will deliver within the Dublin area. Clerys don't send a final list of items purchased.

Congratulations, The Wedding Gift Company, 3 Kylemore Industrial Estate, Killeen Road, Dublin 10, Ph 6232953/4, is the first of its kind in Ireland.

It's an extensive catalogue, with over 2,500 items in the catalogue and the option to add anything you want.

Congratulations usually deliver all of the gifts close to the wedding day, with a complete list of the items purchased and the name and address of the purchaser. The couple can then send off their thank you cards, working from that list.

I talked to Teresa Lavelle mainly to find out if indeed the ubiquitous ironing board was still the

Marry with Taste

priority on the wedding list. She laughed heartily. "When we opened up in 1991 we concentrated on practical items, like toasters, ironing boards, irons, etc but we soon learned a sociological lesson. The Ninties couple are usually in their late twenties or early thirties and they've either been living in flats apart or together. By the time they come to get married now they have acquired a lot of the practical items, either separately or jointly. Now you don't throw out an iron, just because it wasn't a wedding present. What these couples want for wedding presents are accessories and luxury decorative items like crystal and silver. When we first opened we didn't include any silver in the catalogue because we thought no one would want it, now it's one of the biggest sellers. Our most popular range, bought by over ninety per cent of our clients, is the Tudor Mint pewter range of ornaments. Apparently there is a pewter club where these items are bought and sold like stamps in a stamp club."

Garden equipment is another big take which Teresa often has trouble in convincing would-be buyers. "When someone rings up, and they have a particular present in mind, say a dinner service, I often have a hard time trying to convince that person that the couple don't want a dinner service, they want a garden trimmer or a set of garden tools."

Congratulations is essentially a mail order company. I wondered if people didn't mind not having a gift to present.

"Older people often want to collect the present so that they can deliver it themselves and that's OK by us, younger people like having it delivered for them, it saves time, travel, etc."

The Guest/Gift Check List

- Guests Invited To The Wedding Breakfast:

- Name:

- Address:

- Phone:

- Accept:

- Regret:

- Gift:

- Guests Invited to the After Reception:

- Name:

- Address:

- Phone:

- Accept:

- Regret:

- Gift received:

DRESSING THE BRIDE

"I chose my wife, as she did her wedding gown, not for a fine glossy surface, but such qualities as would wear well."
The Vicar of Wakefield, Oliver Goldsmith, 1730-1774

The Stress of Choice

In usage, the word trousseau is synonymous with extravagance when it comes to dressing the bride. I learned from watching the Liz Taylor/Spencer Tracy version of *Father of the Bride*, that trousseau means "a little bundle the bride carries under her arm when she leaves her home!" The search for the wedding dress is akin to the mythological search for the Holy Grail; an almost impossible mission. For like water, water everywhere and not a drop to drink, when it comes to choosing the wedding dress most brides suffer the stress of choice in their search for that something unique and different.

While the fairy-tale extravaganza will always be with us, the current fashion favours cut and classicism above frills and flounces.

Although creams and ivories have become popular in recent years, white, signifying purity of heart and mind, is still the favourite, although ivory is the more flattering shade.

In fact, it was Queen Victoria who set the trend for a white wedding dress, and like herself, it has ruled mightily for a long time.

Rule one. Don't opt for what's fashionable, if the style doesn't suit you. The wedding dress is dateless, nothing is in and nothing is out.

Modern or medieval, the choice is entirely yours. A period dress lends tradition and creates a philosophical mood that captures the essence of eternity. A fringed, Twenties dress makes a bold swinging statement while the coy may want to waft on wings of white muslin. So demure. Whether it's to be understatement or sock 'em in the eye, you must decide. Before you splurge out on swathes of shimmering satin or clouds of chiffon, the burning question is, what is the shape of the body beautiful? If you are tall and willowly with well-sculpted curves, say no more.

Accentuate the Positive

If your body shape is less than hourglass, some consideration must be given to picking a style of dress that will hide the minuses, flaunt the pluses and flatter the better features.

Research shows that the pear-shaped bride—small bust, wide hip—is predominant. Fear not, pear shapes, look to the Victorians who excelled in the art of camouflage. Boned bodices, snugly fit, dropped V-shaped waistlines, gentle tucks and folds falling to the ground, in a virtual contrivance of seams and lines to endow the bust, narrow the waist and hide the hips.

The Art of Masking

* The Short: Long straight lines suggest height, especially a long veil.
* The Beanpole: Break up the line. Ruffles cut, as do tiers, drapes, flounces, frills, fringes, flaps, frippery and furbelows, the options are endless.
* The Large Bosom: Drape or enhance it with an off-the-shoulder style.
* The Flat Bosom: Easy. Padded, boned and bodiced.
* The Thick Waist: Bypass it, either with an empire or

Marry with Taste

H-line. If you must have folds let them fall from the knee.
* The Short Waist: Drop it, the waistline that is, to the hips. A wide cummerbund will effectively lower a slim, repeat, slim, short waist.
* Heavy Hips: Ban bulk, no pleats, gathers, or drapes. The shift shape overlaid with a free flowing layer of chiffon has the twin effect of masking and giving interest.

Think Back

The wedding dress is one of the few fashion items that gets a lot of attention to the back, before the front is properly seen.

If you like simplicity to the front, why not let the detail run riot at the back. The exception is the bride in a wheelchair, for whom back ornamentation is not suitable as it will make the dress uncomfortable.

Think Skin

Is yours a tanned or peaches and cream complexion that will perfectly compliment an off-the-shoulder or scooped neckline? Or is your skin a blotched potched affair that will probably flare up under the stress of the big event? Lace to the face is such a flattering cover-up and veils add a layer of delicate mystery.

Think Scale

Weddings occur in churches, chapels, side altars, registry offices, hotels and homes. The scale of the dress has implications beyond it's clothing purpose. A cathedral-long train needs, you've guessed it, a cathedral-long aisle to take and display its full dimensions. Afterwards, preventing guests from walking on the train can be a problem. Detachable trains allow for the dramatic statement to be made in the morning, without curtailing the high stepping in the afternoon.

Décolleté

A wedding designer tells me that priests have warned that they can refuse to marry the improperly dressed bride! If you decide to marry in a church, it is only reasonable that you pay homage to the full meaning of a religious wedding. See-through skirts and thigh-high slits are a challenge to chastity and should be confined to the honeymoon trousseau.

The Cost

Except, if your budget is unlimited, whether 'tis noble, in the mind's eye, to lash out your lolly in one fell swoop, is the question.

Beatle-like, you may very well say, yeah, yeah, yeah; this is a once in a lifetime occasion, I want my dream dress, on my dream day to be made, my way. Fine. How to achieve that end is the next question. And the good news is, there are a range of options.

Off the Peg Versus the Designer Dress

In Dublin there isn't much difference between the cost of buying a ready-made, off the peg dress and having one specially designed by a wedding dress designer, as you will see from the prices below and as reported by Ann Curtis.

Obviously, the wedding dress designer needs more time than the peg, so it could very well be the planning and organisation, and not so much the money, that'll determine whether you have a shop-made or a specially designed wedding dress.

It also comes down to your own personality and to

Marry with Taste

the way you actually prefer to shop. If you are the type of person who hates looking at patterns/materials/buttons/bows, now is not the time to start. You'd probably prefer to find a dress that you can fit on, know it suits, that it's comfortable, etc. If that's you, shop around, there's plenty of choice.

If, on the other hand, you like to spend time envisaging exactly the sort of dress you'd like to walk up the aisle in, then the wedding dress designer is the route for you. You don't, of course, need to know exactly what you want, the designer will have plenty of ideas and be particularly good at knowing the dress shape that will suit you and even more importantly the shape that won't.

Your most favourite dress, day/debs/sun/cocktail, will provide the vital clue to the style that suits you best. Wear it or bring it with you for your first visit to the dress designer.

Designer Talk

I asked Cora Jakes, wedding dress designer and MD of Jacques Bridal Studio, 12 Malahide Road, Dublin 3, Ph 330173 about the current wedding dress trends in Ireland. Her reply was as definite as it was promptly delivered:

"The fitted sheath dress, sleeveless and bare necked, is in at present. Wonderful for the hourglass brides but hard on the majority."

Cora likes to first see her client at least six months before the wedding. "Most brides are fixated by their shape. I try to tell them that the person inside the body is far more important than the body, but I know that's not what they want to hear. Almost the first thing every bride tells me is that she is going to lose weight.

"A design can range between £200 and £1,000. I supply all the materials because I know what materials make up well and hold their shape without sagging or drooping. It's often difficult for someone not used to buying material to know exactly what material will suit which design.

"I begin the dress seven weeks before the wedding day. It's not a good idea to have the dress ready too early; it can lose its allure. My experience is that most brides lose weight anyway, usually 6/7 lbs, off the waist and diaphragm. Its probably due to pre-marital tension and all of the running around they do. I always make the dress for the figure they are and then, if necessary, tuck it, the week before." Totally unaware, Cora executes one of the most sacred wedding dress traditions of finishing off the dress on the morning of the wedding. It's a superstition that goes back to a time when it was believed that if the dress was finished before the wedding day then the wedding would be called off.

"I like to dress the bride on the morning of the wedding, there's always a final tuck to be made and it's important for me to know that the bride has been perfectly happy with her wedding dress."

Cora's Hot Tip: Expensive delicate materials are easily stained. As well as being clinically clean, never wear make up at a fitting. The slightest smudge of cream, lipstick or mascara can cause havoc.

Patricia Atkins, 20 Carrick Hill Drive, Portmarnock Co Dublin, Ph 8460479, also designs wedding dresses. Her price begins at £120 for a simple design and rises to £800 for an intricate ornate design, all excluding the cost of the material. The cost increases in direct proportion to the amount of appliqué, embroidery and beading required.

While would-be brides can shop around for their own material, Patricia recommends Klara Silks, Deansgrange, Co Dublin, Ph 2894528 (mail order service provided), where raw silk starts at £9 a yard while the heavier silks cost up to £25 a yard and more.

Off the Peg

Hickeys, the fabric and bridal shop, upstairs in Henry Street, Dublin 1, Ph 8730714, has a collection of wedding dresses, some of which are photographed and mounted in a display unit for quick reference.

Prices start at £165 with matching bridesmaids' dresses for the same price. After that the sky and your purse strings are the limit, depending on the level of ornamentation.

Hiring the Haute Couture

If you baulk at the prospect of spending more that the first month's mortgage on your sea of tulle, the option to hire might be better. Then you can have your dream without it turning into a nightmare. When I got married in the late Seventies there were one or two dress hire companies I knew about. Now a glance in the Golden Pages reveals just how much this market has grown.

Again at Hickeys, the wedding dress priced at £165 to buy, can be hired for £65, ditto the matching bridesmaid's dress.

At Annabels, 107 Talbot Street, Ph 8745329, you can hire a wedding dress from £150 to £280, a bridesmaid's dress from £50 to £80 and the flower girl's dress from £35 to £65.

At Delia Bridal, 60a Capel Street, Ph 8734909, wedding dresses range from £80 to £180, they hire out short veils only, for £35 and floral headpieces also cost £35 to hire. At Delia's I'm told the prices are flexible. An overall package deal can be struck to suit the limits of the client's budget.

Delia's also carry a range of dresses aimed at the registry office marriage, the top three-piece ivory suit, skirt, jacket and cami, comes in at £130 to hire.

Crafting the Creation

If you are handy with the needle or have a craft-worker in the family you may decide to tackle the task yourself. As with the designer dress, advance planning and organisation could result in better value for money. On November 1st 1993, when I called into Hickeys in Henry Street, there was no sale on in the shop but upstairs in the Bridal Department, head-dresses were half-price, a beautiful mounted pearl and feather arrangement was down from £40 to £20 as was the most magnificent cream lace material. The message is obvious, buy out of season.

Buy a simple pattern and a material that is easy to work with. Buy a second lot of material to make up a practice dress. Depending on the style, this dummy dress could also be your going-away dress.

Frills, flounces, feathers, buttons, bows, and beads can be added by hand later, to transform what is basically a very simple style into a detailed dramatic effusion. Sewing on beads and bows takes more sweat than skill and gives immense satisfaction.

For a really spectacular finish, borrow some of student, Wendy Hoey's, award-winning ideas. In October 1993, Wendy beat off over twenty contestants to come first in the prestigious International Satzenbrau Designer Competition.

A cane dress was one of her more conservative pieces. You too can add a touch of nature using natural materials, cones, shells, leaves, to make a really original statement, if not on the bridal gown then why not on the bridesmaid's?

Buying Second-hand

The day I went into The Eager Beaver, Crown Alley, Dublin 2, Ph 6773342, to check on their second-hand wedding dresses, I was beaten by the reach of the hand, to the bargain of the year, by a radiant Sian Quill, thrilled to have discovered a perfect regency period wedding dress for £15. Whether Sian will keep it in her "bottom drawer" is undisclosed, her raison d'être for buying it that day was for the the part of the bride in Emma Donoghue's play, *I Know My Own Heart*, at Andrew's Lane Theatre. Some weeks later when I reviewed the play for the *Evening Press* I looked very hard at the dress to see if it looked tatty or second-hand. It didn't. Washed and altered, it looked perfectly charming.

Local Shop

If you are buying a wedding dress in a swop shop in your area, ask if the owner is local. You wouldn't want to walk down the aisle and hear your neighbours proclaim to each other how nice Mary Dunne's dress looks on you! While the shopkeeper probably won't divulge the owner's name, they should and usually do tell if the owner is local or not, it's in their own interests not to place a client in an embarrassing situation.

The Heirloom

Although I'm a hapless hoarder, I've always hated the American tradition of laying out the wedding gown like a corpse and preserving it for posterity in a museum chest.

But now a new restoration service has arrived in Ireland which makes good sense of this practice; the wedding gown can be preserved and passed on to the next generation, see also under Marrying on a Budget.

Lyk-nu Cleaners, 4 The Mall, Donnybrook, Dublin 4, Ph 2692609, have the American franchise on a new method of storing, cleaning, preserving and restoring wedding gowns and various other items of clothing and fabric.

If there's a faded, Miss Haversham's wedding gown in the family that's gone a bit yellow or brown take it to Lyk-nu to have it restored to its original colour. Restoration costs £120, dry cleaning £45.

After the wedding, the dress can once again be treated and stored yet again perhaps for the grandchild of the original owner!

If you come across a really good but faded second-hand dress see if you can come to an arrangement, with the owner, to take it to Lyk-nu to see if it can be restored to its original colour.

The Pregnant Bride

Whoever it was who set the trend for the pregnant bride, perhaps Henry VII, there was a time in recent history when the bride was always preferably pregnant. Fertility was prized as a means to ensure the ancestral line remained intact.

Many of the couples I talked to for this book had been happy to live together outside the bonds of marriage, once they were childless. But with the onset of pregnancy they suddenly, inexplicably, found they wanted to marry, against all of their stated philosophy, mainly for the sake of the child, even though the old concept of illegitimacy is gone.

In fact, one couple who married as soon as the pregnancy was confirmed admitted that they had made such an overt political campaign against marriage, they felt right fools now for wanting to do what they had always said they would not do. Like Thomas Hardy they tried to do it in secret. They cleverly put the notices in the paper "as gaeilge," but were spotted going into the registry office all dressed up. They were mortified with shame to be caught in the act of marriage because they had railed against it for so long, but junior was on the way. The moral is, never say never.

Pregnant brides don't always marry in haste. Very often the pregnancy is planned more with economic constraints in mind than any ethical considerations. The best time for maternity leave, rules OK.

Dressing the pregnant bride is no hassle. White used to symbolise virginity and still can, but not exclusively. A draped dress falling from the shoulders, a tiered tent dress or an empire line from under the bust, will all allow plenty of room for the bride to blossom on her big day. Everything else is as usual.

Shoes

Nothing becomes a wedding dress quite so much as matching covered shoes. Dorans, Millbourne Avenue, Dublin 9, Ph 367222, have been covering shoes since 1931; they also cover shoes for people with special requirements.

Costs:

* Shoe covering: £13.50
* Bows: £4
* Lace and double coverings: £18
* Slingbacks: £16

Wedding Dress Checklist

✍ Name, address, Phone Contact/Designer:

✍ To be ready:

✍ Price agreed:

✍ Material selected:

✍ Hoop:

✍ Applique, beading, embroidery:

✍ First fitting:

✍ Second fitting:

✍ Final fitting:

ACCESSORIES

❦

Veiled or Unveiled?

"Even forms and substances are circumfused,
By that transparent veil with light divine;"
The Prelude, Wordsworth, 1850

The blusher veil dates back to the time when the hunter snared his bride in much the same way as he snared his foxes, in a sack, which was then used to carry the treasure home. Remember *Seven Brides for Seven Brothers* ? In time a compromise was reached and the sack was replaced by the blusher veil, now an anachronism.

But for those with a penchant for the dramatic touch, the blusher veil offers plenty of scope. The mystique and allure of the covered face on arrival at church is in such contrast to the theatrical triumphant post-vow throw-back culminating in the revelation of the bride beautiful. Performances vary.

Whether you decide on the blusher veil, the spectacular trailing cloud of veiling or a Virgin Mary-type understated, tidied away affair, remember the colour must match the dress and remember too that dazzling white can make its wearer look a whiter shade of pale. Compensate with a darker shade of make up or choose ivory which flatters everyone.

Lyk-nu can also restore veils, so again it might be worth while to check the relatives' attics!

The Head-dress/Headpiece

Veils can be held in place with an alice band, a halo of

fresh or silk flowers or a headpiece. Except for the floral arrangement, these can all be hired but make sure to check the shop price before hiring, it may be cheaper to buy depending on exactly what you want.

I used a head hugging Juliet cap and was surprised to find my husband calling me Jessica (from *The Merchant of Venice*) all day.

Skull-hugging Juliet caps are easy to make in the same material as the wedding dress, as mine was, and adorned with beading, brambles or embroidery.

As you're going to be Queen Bee for a day, why not a tiara, à la Princess Di?

You can always wear a head-dress without a veil but since this may be the very last time you can seriously take to the tulle, can you really turn down such an opportunity?

Interlaced ribbons and flowers with a plaited hairstyle look very cool and take height from a tall bride; conversely, a solitary rose lends height.

If you are carrying a bouquet, then parasols, gloves and bags will only cause clutter. If in doubt, leave them out.

Lingerie

The sheath dress requires an assortment of equally sheath, svelte underwear to avoid the undesirable VPLS, visible panty line syndrome. Silk is always desirable, but if unaffordable, the chain stores all have an excellent range of good quality, fake silk underwear.

To avoid last minute panics, buy the bra, the slip and the panties before the first fitting of the wedding dress and thereafter wear them for every fitting. Straps, and lace peekaboos are a no-no. So is a darker shade shining through, match the under to the outerwear.

If in olden days a piece of stocking was looked on as something shocking, then so are pop socks today. They look awful when the bride flashes the "something blue" garter at the video camera. Lace bridal tights add the final touch of luxury. At Roches Stores and Brown Thomas from £5.

Jewellery

If your dress is plain then you can make a bold statement with your jewellery. It doesn't have to be expensive, as you know from the Maupassant story.

If the dress is ornate with beading and sequins then the jewellery is best understated.

A simple string or two, or three, of pearls, with matching earrings is understated elegance at its most serene. Pearls are a good buy because it's not easy to define how cultured or uncultured they are with the naked eye. If you don't like jewellery don't wear it, with so many other adornments it won't be missed.

Getting into Shape

> "One hundred years should go to praise,
> Thine eyes and on thy forehead gaze,
> Two hundred to adore each breast,
> But thirty thousand to the rest,
> An age at least to every part,
> And the last age should show your heart"
> *To His Coy Mistress,* Andrew Marvell

There is one very effective way of getting in shape and the good news is it costs absolutely nothing, but willpower.

Nothing, no expensive skin cream, no lotions, or magic potions, can come within an ass's roar of the powerful triangle of a wholesome diet, regular exercise, and plenty of "sleep, that knits the ravelled sleeve of care." Up your intake of water, fruit and vegetables, cut your intake of fat and sugary foods. Walk, swim or cycle for at least thirty minutes, at least three times a week, and, sleepwise, the hour before midnight works wonders.

If practised over a sufficiently long period, this routine will result in a slimmer, trimmer, positively glowing new you.

If preferred, join a gym and work out gently, but don't be too strenuous, you don't want to pull anything vital.

Alternative Medicine

George Bernard Shaw said that if a man/woman is not his/her own doctor by the time they are forty then they are fools.

You don't have to wait until forty to become your own medic. Start early by taking preventive steps rather than waiting until you need a cure.

Alternative medicine offers plenty of scope to actively fend off illnesses. Very few people get through the pre-nuptials without at some stage feeling totally stressed out.

Ki-massage, reflexology and acupuncture do for the body what the starting motor does for the car, it gets you up and running.

Ki-massage is a massage technique which relaxes both the mind and body, relieves stress, tension, fatigue. Combined with aromatherapy the total effect is one of soothing serenity.

The foot is said to be the map of the body. In reflexology the foot is masssaged in a particular way to stimulate the energy channels, induce relaxation and prevent illness. Every time I get reflexology I feel like I'm walking on clouds for at least two days.

Acupuncture is a Chinese medicine in which needles are inserted into the skin as therapy for various disorders, including asthma, arthritis, and insomnia. Acupuncture works so well it can and has been used successfully as an anaesthetic for dental purposes, surgical operations and caesarian sections.

Perhaps the real plus of all these treatments is that as well as curing and fending off illnesses, they can be used simply as a means of inducing well-being, balance and harmony for both the mind and body.

Treatments take thirty to sixty minutes and cost from £10 to £20 per session.

Make Up

At Ultima One in Swords, Ph 8404278, you can have your hair blow-dryed and a full face make up for £12, with an extra charge of £2 for an up style. A full manicure will cost £8 while a file and paint only routine is £4.50. A half-leg wax is £10, full leg-wax £18.

A full facial, usually executed three to four days before the wedding costs from £12 to £20.

Many beauticians also provide a home service. Obviously you'd need to try out the make up service at least once before the wedding day.

The majority of brides apply their own make up, with a little bit of help from the bridesmaid. The balance between looking natural in the daylight and yet having sufficient make up on for the video camera is a difficult one to strike. And all the whites can have a very draining effect on the natural colour of the face. A light tan is always the preferred option but if you haven't got a natural colour from all the walking, cycling and swimming as outlined above, don't be tempted to take sun-beds.

Look at the statistics on the increase of skin cancer in Ireland and talk to any skin cancer specialist for two minutes, they simply say a blanket no to all sunbeds. The intelligent, informed woman wears false boobs and fake tan.

Getting back to make up. Check well in advance that you have enough make up to last at least until the honeymoon is over. You don't want to be poking the last bit of your favourite lipstick out of its holder with a hairpin on the morning of your wedding, now do you?

Mascara is the one thing that causes lots of black smudges at weddings, and not just for the bride. I don't cry very often in real life, but there's something about wedding music that gets my tap running. I howled my way through every second of my own wedding ceremony and when it was over I was glad I had worn water-proof mascara; Outdoor Girl. It was indeed water-proof.

If you don't normally wear mascara don't let anyone persuade you to wear it on your wedding day. I know of a bride who did just that and she was blinking so much she had to remove it before she could sign the register.

Hands and Nails

When you think about it, the wedding day is probably the one and only day in all our lives when our hands get so much attention, what with the joining of hands, the inspection of the new rings, cutting the cake, and the close-up photographs of the precious moments, our digits need to be displayed with dignity and decorum. Nibbled nails, chewed cuticles, and nicotine-stained fingers do not make a pretty picture. If you can bear it, put on plenty of hand cream, Vaseline or oil, last thing at night and sleep with gloves on for several weeks preceding your wedding. Keep cuticles in good condition, file nails with an emery board and wear nail varnish to keep the nails strong.

The night before the wedding, when you go to bed, apply two coats of varnish, join hands, fingers interlocked to prevent smudging and sleep peacefully.

The Accessories Checklist

✍ Shoes:

✍ Underwear:

✍ Make up/Jewellery:

✍ Head-dress:

✍ Headpiece:

✍ Veil:

✍ Massage booked:

✍ Reflexology session booked:

✍ Acupuncture appointment:

✍ Make up session booked:

✍ Hair appointment:

✍ Make up, oils and sprays:

✍ Nail varnish:

✍ Emery boards:

✍ Creams:

DRESSING THE GROOM...FROM TOPPER TO TOE

"But for his funeral train
Which the bridegroom sees in the distance,
Would he so joyfully, think you,
Fall in with the marriage-procession?"
Amours de Voyage, Arthur Hugh Clough,
1819-1861

Luckily for all brides, most grooms don't take quite such a doomed view of marriage, even though they have been very much cast in the baddie role! For if the bride signalled her purity by wearing white, then surely the tradition of obliging the groom to wear black was a terrible indictment on the state of his soul! Never mind the fact that many grooms enjoy wearing black, it's the why of it that seems so presumptuous.

"Be not the first by which the new is tried,
Nor yet the last to leave the old aside."

Happily, today's groom can take Milton's advice and try something new, maybe even marry all in white. Isn't that the real dilemma for the groom who wants to wear the traditional suit in order to do the right thing but feels he will be uncomfortable in what is dubbed, the monkey suit? All is not lost. I always thought that the range of bridal clothes for men was something akin to the range of Henry Ford's cars; any colour once it's black.

In fact, the selection of colours and styles now available to the groom is staggering, not to mention elegant.

Marry with Taste

The rule is, almost anything goes for the groom, although the Nineties has seen a great swing back to formal wear.

The adventurous groom will delight in the white single-breasted tuxedos, worn with black evening trousers with pleats or dress stripe that are now in fashion. 1993 saw the launch of the full white wedding suit in lightweight material. For bright sparks, of course! Self-patterned green and navy jackets, worn with black trousers, are another new addition to the wedding scene, aimed mainly at the younger groom.

The slightly adventurous groom can have a traditionally-styled morning suit in a woven material that gives it a very new Nineties look.

The traditional groom has a choice of morning suits, grey tails in fine pure wool and frock coats in black, worn always with grey check or stripe tie or cravat with a breast pocket handkerchief to match.

The shirt should be plain white or with a self-stripe and double cuff; the wing collar should be worn with a cravat. Lace-up shoes and silk or cotton socks, also black. Gloves and top hat in black or grey to match the favoured six-button double-breasted waistcoat.

The new navy frock coat, with coordinating silver-blue waistcoats and morning trousers, worn with a wing-collared shirt and a navy cravat is particularly fetching. Grey top hat and gloves completes the look.

Or you could say it in silver, with a silver grey three-piece morning suit, complemented by a grey or navy tie and completed with grey hat and gloves.

The semi-morning suit comprises a black lounge jacket with grey waistcoat and striped morning trousers, worn with a shirt and tie. Since the more favoured time to get married has changed from morning to the afternoon, fashion has followed and despite its title morning dress is not only popular, it's absolutely PC for the afternoon ceremony.

I believe the gleaming black silk top casts a funereal

presence on a wedding. It makes me think about that scene in Ulysses where James Joyce's character, Bloom, attends the famous funeral at Glasnevin attired in full regalia, including the black bowler.

The grey topper is much in evidence, with white gloves; the latter are not meant to be worn, just carried for effect. The hat is usually only worn for the photographs. The best man must take care of the groom's topper in the church and make sure no one sits on it.

The vast majority of men hire their wedding suit. In the market place, demand creates supply. The good news for the groom is, there's a huge range of dress-hire companies for men, much more than for women, and they are usually no further than the local shopping centre.

Don't look at the catalogue, look at the clothes; have two fittings, one when booking, one the day before the wedding. Before you leave the dress-hire company, check carefully for wear and tear so that you cannot be accused of causing damage which was there when you collected the item.

Ideally, the bride and groom make the joint decision about the sort of wedding they want, formal or informal. If a disagreement arises, since the bride has the choice of whatever dress she wants, then the groom should have the wedding suit of his choice, it's his special day too!

Unless he chooses something spectacularly outlandish, like a foppish artist's outfit replete with French beret (counselling could help), the groom will be to the bride as foliage is to the flower, a decorative accessory, giving solid support, all the better to let her shine brightest.

One of the advantages of the formal morning suit, as against the latest fashion outfit, is that the formal morning suit is timeless, it never goes out of style and therefore will look good in photographs in fifty years.

I was at a wedding where the groom, expecting to be something of a sensation, wore the dress coat and

Marry with Taste

tails worn by his father at his wedding. Nobody even noticed!

On the other hand, if you look at wedding albums from the Seventies, with the men wearing the latest, yard-wide bell bottoms, you want to fall around laughing!

In the end, it's really down to the personality of the groom whether he goes for the most fashionable lounge suit or the formal outfit, always bearing in mind the style of the wedding that the couple have in mind.

If the groom wants to be suave and smart in a morning suit he has tradition and fashion on his side. But you must be able to wear it, and even more importantly, so must the ushers, the best men and the two fathers. There is nothing more awful than to watch a bridal party with the men strutting round in morning suits like demented ducks because they feel out of water. Even the way they walk is a real giveaway.

The time of year has a bearing on the groom's attire. Dark colours and heavy materials look warm and comfortable in winter and often are a better match if the bride is wearing a heavy brocade or velvet.

In summer the bright suit and silk morning suits in pale grey tone in very well with the bridal silks and chiffons.

Nowadays there's a baffling range of morning suits to choose from, in grey, black and navy in a huge variety of shades in silks and wools and woven materials. If you want to create a well-to-do impression, nothing beats the traditional black tailcoat, charcoal trousers (grey with stripe), grey waistcoat, wing-collared white shirt, grey cravat, grey top hat, white gloves, black socks and shoes. Pale grey trousers can be worn instead of the charcoal trousers if desired. Remember, watch the handkerchief, if it clashes with the lapel flower, remove it.

Mixing and matching works if carefully planned. If the groom and the best man want to wear full morning dress but find the fathers reluctant, the dress-hire companies have a selection of lounge suits that have been designed and cut to fit in with the style of the morning dress.

Informal lounge suits can be worn with a white or coloured shirt. The latter looks better if it tones in with the colours of the bridal party. Waistcoats have made great strides these last few years. The sombre black and dull grey have given way to bright and muted multi-coloureds, rich cherries and golden yellows. Brocade waistcoats are particularly good in winter, especially if the bride is in velvet.

For the fully informal wedding, while the men don't need to wear matching suits, it's obviously best if all of the bridal party are in a similar shade, either dark or light, whether that's blue, brown, charcoal or cream.

Comedians like Brendan Grace, Brendan Carroll, and Dermot Morgan have brought braces back in fashion and with the braces and the tie the groom can make a colourful statement, which should tone in with the colours the bridesmaids are wearing.

No freshly scalped hair-dos. The groom should have his hair cut three weeks in advance. No hobbling either. New shoes should be broken in weeks before too.

Blacktie—6763126/8743312—the biggest gentlemen's outfitters in Ireland, suggests the following accessories:

For Formal Wear:

* White shirt or neatly striped with white collar and double cuffs. For very formal weddings a white shirt is a must but a brighter stripe may be acceptable. The shirt collar is normally of a standard shape but a white wing collar is sometimes worn.
* Tie: Silk grey check or striped. Club and regimental ties are also worn if they match with the rest of the outfit. If a wing collar is worn then a cravat in the same colour as the tie is worn.
* Bow ties are not worn with morning wear.

Marry with Taste

* Waistcoat: Black is never incorrect. Grey is more popular as are coloured waistcoats in camel and brocade. Waistcoats can be single or double-breasted, backless with elastic attachment or full back.
* Socks: Black silk or fine cotton.
* Shoes: Never, never any other colour except black, preferably lace-up.
* Handkerchief: In breast pocket to coordinate with tie. Be warned: the amount of the handkerchief showing reflects how extrovert the wearer is!
* Gloves: Black or grey kid or cotton to match waistcoat.
* Hat: Black or grey to match waistcoat.
* Cummerbunds: Match the bow and should be pleated with a small pocket in the pleat. Cummerbunds are particularly useful when worn with a shirt with a laid-on front, as they mask the bottom of the front which could otherwise show above the waistband.

Also available:

* Shirts: Plain white with conventional collar. Plain wing collar with fly front. Dress wing collar with double cuff. Conventional collar with dress front and double cuff.
* Bow ties, cummerbunds and handkerchiefs: Regular and slim sizes, in a variety of shades, perhaps made specially to match material in bridesmaid's dress.
* Cravats: Grey and pastels, held with a pearl stick-pin.
* Dress scarfs: Usually, though nor exclusively, for evening wear.
* Cuff links: Gold, silver, mother of pearl, diamond cut.
* Top hats: Ascot grey and black silk
* Gloves: White or grey.

Checklist for the Groom.

- Name, address and phone:

- Contact:

- Price agreed:

- Type of suit for groom/bestman:

- Style of suit for fathers:

- When to collect:

- Will clothes be collected/delivered afterwards:

- Will there be a charge for this service:

- Who will organise the return of clothes:

- Who will bring groom's going-away outfit to reception venue:

HOW YOU CAN SAY IT WITH...FLOWERS

❦

"Where'er you walk, cool gales shall fan the glade,
Trees, where you sit, shall crowd into a shade:
Where'er you tread, the blushing flowers shall rise,
And all things flourish where you turn your eyes."
Pastorals, Alexander Pope

Three hundred years later and Alexander Pope's sentiments on flower power are still perfectly valid. Nothing can create the visual ambience, the tangible freshness, the sense that "all things will flourish" on this very special day, as succinctly or powerfully as flowers.

Just as the bride is indisputably the focal picture on the wedding day, so are the flowers, the frame, the resonating factor that gives a visual cohesion to the entire wedding party from the home, to the church or registry office to the reception. Even the guest bus can be thematically bedecked!

Although I chose the day myself (my matron of honour doubling up as the florist), Monday is not a big wedding day in Ireland. Flowers either have to be made up as a special, and therefore more expensive, Sunday order or be made on Saturday and nursed over the weekend.

Traditionally, flowers symbolise fertility. So, in the strict sense of the word, should the career-minded bride, not intending to procreate, carry a bouquet at all? Yes, is the answer. It's her day and old traditions must adapt to new times.

If marriage is bondage (albeit, entered willingly by

both parties), then a well-placed arrangement of leafy frondage can work on an allegorical as well as a visual level. All the intertwining of floral stems and verdant foliage are a perfect metaphor for the couple's fresh and new, united-yet-individual, status of the bride and groom.

What Flowers Say

Like the gems in the engagement ring, flowers have a silent language.

Red roses	*love*
Tulips	*declarations of love*
Scarlett poppies	*great extravagance*
Red poppies	*consolation*
White lily	*purity*
Hyacinth	*sport*
Violet	*faithfulness*
{ Honeysuckle	
Gypsophilia	*fidelity*
Ivy	
Orange Blossom	*pregnant bride/fertility*
Lilac	*first love*
Carnation	*pure love*
Forget-me-not	*true love*
White chrysanthemum	*truth*

Who Pays?

From the simplest single flower arrangement to the overwhelming abundant bowery, the choice is wide open, confined, as usual, only by budgetary constraints.

Traditionally, the bride's family paid for the flowers in the church and at the reception and the groom's family paid for the rest.

Nowadays the groom pays for all flowers.

Marry with Taste

Choosing the Bouquet

Do you like singled-headed flowers or sheaves? Retiring or resplendent colours? Flowers that float or flowers that stand to attention? The choice is as long as a length of ivy!

Unless you intend going for a very simple casual look, floristry is the one area of the wedding accessories best left to the experts. It's a time-consuming, skilled task that must be carried out at the last minute when lots of other last minute items will also be demanding attention.

A well-thought-out floral arrangement can draw all the visual threads of your wedding picture together for maximum visual impact.

Remember, the flowers will be in every photograph so they'll need to stand up to inspection.

For many people, other than picking up a bunch of flowers at the supermarket, or a potted plant at the garden centre, ordering the flowers for their wedding will be the first time in their lives to visit a professional florist. So how can you suddenly design a bouquet?

Get inspiration from florist's portfolios and scour the bridal magazines for new trends and ideas. You may know already what sort of bouquet you want, fresh, dried or silk, but the shape and size of your bouquet, the variety and size of the flowers you choose, and whether the bouquet should be formal or informal are all variables that must be decided on.

There are no hard and fast rules, but if the bridal dress is cut on simple classical lines then a strong bold statement can be made with flowers, while an ornate dress will be better enhanced by a simple bouquet.

Popular Bouquet Shapes

* The triangular shower/teardrop/cascade bouquet, comes long or short, and is the most popular choice of

bridal bouquet.
* The crescent bouquet has a small central posy with two points.
* The waterfall has three points, a central posy, plus a long central point and a short matching point, each side.
* The colonial posy is a large circular posy of generous-sized flowers. Trailing ribbons and foliage are an optional extra. This posy is especially suited to a Victorian-style dress.
* The actress Nell Gwyn immortalised the flat basket bouquet.
* The pom-pom is a ball-shaped posy ideal for small children.

Colours

Red, orange and yellow are the colours associated with vibrancy and liveliness. Blue, purple and most dark colours are cool and formal for the classic look but can very easily recede.
Bouquets are best either multi-coloured or as a single "saturation" colour. Red against white is startling. Peach against white is beguiling. Blue against white has a reverential appeal.

The Size of the Blooms

Large: Large flowers, like orchids, roses and carnations take centre stage and look best with leafy greenery, fern or foliage.
Medium: Medium or fill flowers can be used to give contrast and perhaps complete the colour scheme, lilies and freesia being the most popular, although freesia as a stand-alone bouquet is also particularly popular for the bridesmaids' posies.
Small: Small flowers are used to soften the edges of what would otherwise be too solid an arrangement,

Marry with Taste

Gypsophilia and leaves are especially popular.

The Size of the Bouquet

The height of the bride and the scale of the dress and wedding should be borne in mind when deciding on the size of the bouquet. Slender, elongated bouquets are meant to flatter brides with broad hips! A petite bride should not be burdened by a overweight bouquet while a very tall bride can carry trailing ivy to good effect.

Now you know what flowers, colour, size and shape you'd like your bouquet to be, take a piece of the material from both the bridal and bridesmaid's dress to the florist, get professional advice on what matches what and make an informed decision.

Groom, Bride's Father, Groom's Father, Best Man and Ushers
 Usually white non-droop carnations.

Bride's Mother and Groom's Mother
 The two mothers usually wear exactly the same corsage of orchids or roses.

Bridesmaids
 The choice ranges from the formal bouquet, through a nosegay, a basket of flowers, pom-poms, to sheaves and single flowers.

Young attendants
 Tinies get bored so quickly. Don't risk a forgotten bouquet or basket, better to include their flowers either as a floral hairband or sewn into their outfits; hem garlands—front only—are deliciously eye-catching.

Church Flowers

Will there be two weddings? If so, it might be easier on the day, and cheaper, to liaise with the other wedding party and see if it would be possible to agree on a neutral colour scheme that would suit both weddings and share the expenses. A sympathetic priest or minister will either provide the necessary details or act as go-between.

The regular and often voluntary church florist will usually be delighted to supply an arrangement of flowers for an agreed fee. For the church, a bold rather than an intricate arrangement, placed in a high well-lit area is best as the flowers have to be seen from the back, as well as the front, of the church. White and creams demand attention, dark colours recede.

Pew ends can really set the aisle aglow for that important entrance but unless the church can supply suitable containers, pew ends can be very expensive. Perhaps a series of colour-coordinated bows could be used instead, tied on the end of each row of pews.

Reception Flowers

If the reception is being held at a hotel or in a local banqueting hall, the floral arrangements are usually part of the deal, unless you want a particular thematic scheme.

Cake Top

Again, colour coordinated fresh flowers have replaced the bride/groom statues.

Best Selling Bouquets: Merna O'Neill of the Flower Bowl, 11 Orwell Road, Rathgar, Dublin 6, Ph 4978741, tells me that very few flowers are ever out of season because most of the flowers on sale are imported from

Marry with Taste

Holland. Ninety per cent of her brides walk up the aisle carrying roses, the most popular bouquet being the shower. Throwing the bouquet is also on the wane. Many brides have the flowers of the bouquet pressed into a dried picture to keep for evermore.

Having the Bouquet Pressed and Framed

Ann's Pressed Bouquet Pictures, 64 Newcourt Road, Bray, Co Wicklow, Ph 2862890.

Ann Corcoran likes to get the bouquet as soon as possible after the wedding. "I take the bouquet apart and make it into a picture, in a bouquet shape, and then frame it. The wedding invitation, a photograph or the menu can also be included. The average cost for a bride's bouquet in a 12 x 14 inch frame is £50. The bridesmaid's bouquet is around £30, for an 8 x 10 inch frame, while the mother's corsage costs £7.50 for a tiny 3.5 x 4 inch frame. They are meant as momentos. Because the orchid turns mahogany brown I cut it down and surround it with the freesia. The process takes about three months."

The Floral Checklist

- Florist: Name, address, phone:

- Contact:

- Details agreed for bride's bouquet:

- Details for bride's head-dress/parasol:

- Bridesmaids:

- Flower girl/page boy:

- Corsages: Mother of Bride and Groom:

- Buttonholes for Groom, Fathers, Best Man, ushers:

- Church flowers:

- Reception flowers:

- Flowers to be collected/delivered:

- Agreed price/to be paid:

The Wedding Cake

"She tells enough white lies to ice a wedding cake."
Said by Margot Asquith, Countess of Oxford & Asquith, about Lady Desborough, published in *The Listener* in 1953.

Pishogues and Customs

It was in ancient Rome that the tradition of the rich cake for the wedding breakfast began. Like flowers, it symbolises the hope of fruitfulness and fertility. Home-bakers beware, no finger licking the mixing bowl since tradition has it that tasting the cake before the wedding could cause a bride to lose her husband's love. Did you ever wonder why the bride and groom cut the cake together? It wards off infertility!

Spinsters and bachelors who attend the wedding and then sleep with a piece of cake under the pillow will dream of their future partner. A tier of the wedding cake is often held over for the first anniversary or christening but that custom may be derivative of another custom when slices of the wedding cake of the first married are kept until all of the females in the family have found partners. If this is not done, the daughters risk spinsterhood.

Pishogues apart, the wedding cake, having centre stage in front of the bride and groom, is a focal point of the reception. Indeed, the cake often stands alone on a table swagged with garlands of flowers and lit by an overhead spotlight.

If Victorians developed the wedding cake into an architectural art form, the Americans began the two wedding cake custom. Yes, in America as well as getting photographed two weeks before the wedding, in some states the tradition is to have two wedding cakes. One cake is for the groom, his favourite of course, chocolate or whatever, that's served at the rehearsal dinner. The bride sticks with the traditional fruit cake and that's preserved for the real wedding! Wedding cakes can be cut with knives specially engraved for the occasion, ceremonial daggers called dirks, or at military weddings, swords or sabres.

The Size

How many tiers you'll need depends on the number of guests at the wedding, the number of people who cannot attend the wedding, but to whom you may want to give a slice later and if you intend keeping a tier for the first christening or anniversary, which ever comes first. Like wine, a fruit cake improves with age once it gets a regular sup of spirits skewered into it. In general, the three-tier is the norm, with a 25 cm tier serving eighteen, a 30 cm twenty-two/thirty-four. The width of the slice will determine the yield per tier.

The Shape

The traditional, three-tiered, round/square, rich fruit cake covered with royal icing is giving way to horse shoes, initials, and novel shapes reflecting the couple's lifestyle and interests: a tennis racket shape, or the fifth tee of the local golf club. Sponge and chocolate confections also make delicious alternatives.

Cakes can be ordered from a bakery, or a professional confectioner. There is a big tradition in Ireland for the cake to be made at home; my mother made mine and then had it iced professionally. It's considered bad luck for the bride to make her own.

When making a tiered cake get the tier proportions right, so that the pyramid is balanced. Large tiers are tricky to cook. Allow a one-inch space between the oven walls and the tin.

Cake Decorations or Toppers

Flowers/Bride/Groom statues/Cherubs/Bells/Shells/Token Items.

In 1993 a vet from Swords presented his future father-in-law with two Charollais heifers as a "dowry" while asking for the hand of his daughter, Susan, in marriage. This theme was continued when the couple were represented on the wedding cake as two formally dressed cattle!

The topper on the cake can be used to recall where the couple met, a ballroom of romance, or shells for a beach. Or it can allude to where the couple are heading. No doubt in 1994, what with Ireland being in the World Cup, we'll see a proliferation of football toppers, indicating a USA-bound honeymoon.

Current Trends

Patrick O'Reilly of Celebration Cakes, Ph 921216, the only professional cake maker in the 1993 Golden Pages, says:

"The three-tiered rich fruit cake, covered in royal icing, is on the way out. The staggered cake, set up on metal stands, one over the other, in E and S arrangements, has replaced it. The rich fruit cake mixture is often confined to one tier with a light fruit mixture in the other tiers. The most popular icing now is fondant icing; it's a much softer icing. It's best to make the cake six months before the wedding, it matures nicely. Three days before the wedding day, the cake is iced. I can match any colours. But the fondant icing doesn't keep as well as royal icing and it loses its colour. The stronger colours fade and the pale colours change to ivory. If a tier is being kept for the first anniversary or christening we replace the fondant icing with royal icing."

A Celebration cake I saw at a wedding fair owed more to architecture than cookery for its appearance. The main centre cake was arranged above a miniature pink waterfall; linking bridges joined the two smaller tiers.

Karen Heffernan is a prize-winning confectioner with Manning's Bakery, Ph 8477236. Karen took first place in the one tier Batex Wedding Cake Competition in 1993 and her black cake, covered with white orchids, took fourth place in the Batex Theme Wedding Cake Competition. In 1992 she baked and iced 138 cakes and in the first nine months of 1993 the number had risen to 200!

Like Patrick O'Reilly she has noticed a shift away from the traditional three-tiered, rich fruit cake:

"As well as baking and icing cakes from scratch, I get a lot of sponges and fruit cakes to ice. But some of the cakes don't stand up to handling and fall apart in the box, in transport. It's a problem but we can patch it up before the icing goes on."

The moral of that story is, if you make your own cake, be careful how you pack it when it's going to the confectioner for icing.

My mother baked many delicious wedding cakes for the family, myself and cousins included, using this recipe:

Cake Recipe

The Six-Inch Square

4 oz	plain flour
3 1/2 oz	brown sugar
3 1/2 oz	butter or margarine
1 3/4 lbs	dried fruit

Marry with Taste

1 1/2 oz	glacé cherries
1 1/2 oz	whole almonds
1 1/2 oz	mixed peel
1 oz	ground almonds
3	size 3 eggs
3/4	level teaspoon of mixed spice
1/4	level teaspoon of nutmeg
1	tiny pinch of ground clove
1	dessertspoon of caramel or treacle
	grated rind of 1/2 lemon
1/2	glass of spirits. (If cake is to be stored, 1 glass of spirits)
	small pinch of bread soda, if using caramel
1/4	level teaspoon of salt

This tier is often stored. It will keep well for two years or more. Add one extra glass of spirits in addition to the amount given in recipe. The mixture is a fraction richer and therefore will keep well and be moist even if stored for some time.

The Eight Inch square

10 oz	plain flour
8 oz	brown sugar
8 oz	butter or margarine
2 lbs & 2 oz	dried fruit
3 1/2 oz	glacé cherries
3 1/2 oz	whole almonds
3 1/2 oz	mixed peel
2 1/2 oz	ground almonds
6	eggs
1 3/4	level teaspoon of mixed spice
1/2	level teaspoon of nutmeg
1	tiny pinch of ground clove
1	tablespoon of caramel or treacle
	grated rind of medium-sized lemon

3/4	glass of spirits
1/4	teaspoon of bread soda, if using caramel
1/2	level teaspoon of salt

The Ten-Inch Square

14 oz	plain flour
12 oz	butter or margarine
12 oz	brown sugar
3 1/2 lbs	dried fruit
5 oz	glacé cherries
5 oz	whole almonds
5 oz	mixed peel
4 oz	ground almonds
2	tablespoons of caramel or treacle
	grated rind of one lemon
	small pinch of ground clove
8	eggs
1	glass of spirits or water
1	dessertspoon of mixed spice
3/4	level teaspoon of nutmeg
1/2	level teaspoon of bread soda, if using caramel
1	level teaspoon of salt

Instructions

You will need a big bowl.

1. Remove stalks from fruit. Clean and dry.
2. Rinse and dry glacé cherries.
3. Sift flour and spices together, add grated lemon rind.
4. Cream butter and add in sugar, by hand or with food mixer.
5. Beat eggs in, alternating with small amounts of flour from the allocated amount to prevent mixture curdling.
6. When all the eggs are beaten in, fold in the rest of the flour.

7. Add fruit, nuts, spirits, caramel or treacle.
8. Spoon the mixture, which should be stiff and not too wet.

How to Line a Baking Tin

Treble-line tins to avoid all danger of scorch.
Allow:
3 1/2 to 3 3/4 hours for 6" cake. Reduce heat after 10 minutes.
4 1/2 to 4 3/4 hours for 8" cake. Reduce heat after 20 minutes.
5 to 5 1/2 hours for 10" cake. Reduce heat after 40 minutes.
Test before removing from oven.
Small cakes need careful baking.
Cool all cakes for a short time in tin, then turn out on wire tray.
Allow twelve hours to cool before wrapping in double folds in greaseproof paper or foil.
Strip off lining papers while the cake is still just warm or they could be hard to remove later when you will be in danger of damaging cake.

Make the cake at least four months in advance so that it has plenty of time to mature before taking it to the professional confectioner for icing.

The Cake Checklist

- Name, address, phone of confectioner:
- Contact:
- No. of tiers:
- Type of cake:
- Type of icing:
- Colour and decoration:
- How will the cake be displayed:
- Delivered to:
- Date:
- Stands to be returned or collected:
- Agreed price:

The Transportation

"Did ye not hear it? No: 'twas but the wind
Or the car rattling o'er the stony street
On with the dance! let joy be unconfined;
No sleep till morn, when Youth and Pleasure meet
To chase the glowing Hours with flying feet."
Childe Harold's Pilgrimage, Lord Byron.

Whether you want to sock 'em in the eye with a stretch limo, dazzle them with a Daimler, evoke sentimental ohs and ahs with a horse-drawn bridal brougham, or rattle o'er the stony street in your own old banger, the choice of transport is huge, bound only by the budget.

For many brides the wedding car from which to wave graciously and entertain the bystanders is an essential part of the thrill of the wedding day. The need for room for the bridal gown and head-dress is the justification for this expensive accessory, but the big car really comes into the if-they-could-see-me-now syndrome, the transport aspect is secondary.

Most of the wedding car services offer four trips ranging from £75 to £150, its well worth shopping around.

First collected is the groom, provided he lives within a specified distance of the bride's home, around twenty miles. Then the bridesmaids, followed by the bride and her father. And sometimes, just for the fun of it, mother comes too. After the ceremony the bridal car takes the newly-weds from the church or registry office to the reception. This trip can include a stop-off to a rose garden, or the photographers studio, or the sea, or perhaps to visit a close relative in hospital.

The wedding car of today offers a lot more than transport—the cocktail cabinet stocks, replete with ice box, wine, beer, sparkling champagne, while the TV ensures that you needn't miss your favourite soap just because it's your wedding day! Ugh. Nor need you sacrifice that vital business call just to get married, the ubiquitous mobile telephone is available on request. The traditional big black car has almost had its sell-by date. White or cream are the favoured colours with sumptuous-sounding shades like regency bronze, champagne gold, Georgian silver, midnight blue and royal burgandy gaining ground, so to speak.

Current Trends: Robert Lynch brought the first stretch limo to the Irish wedding market in August 1993. "It's a 23 1/2 foot long five litre Lincoln Towncar, an incredibly luxurious limousine. It costs £150 for a wedding. This includes a uniformed chauffeur and to really make the bride feel like Cinderella going to the ball, an (optional) footman. There's a complimentary bar, TV, video, stereo and solid screen between the couple and the driver to ensure total privacy."

Robert admits that the service is used mainly by young, image-conscious couples who want to make a splash on their big day.

Contact Robert at American Classic Limousines, Swords, Co Dublin, Ph 8406022/088 532691.

Visually, the open carriage, evoking the pomp and pagentry of kings and queens down through the ages, is particularly attractive. In practice, it has its disadvantages. If the day turns suddenly bad, the bride risks arriving at the church with a wrecked hairstyle, ruined make-up and a rainy-look dress, not exactly a pretty picture. Vintage cars look arrestingly different and the fun you'll have waving to the neighbours and the passers-by will look especially picturesque when captured on video, as would the horse and carriage.

Marry with Taste

In both of these modes of transport ask the driver—James, who else!—to take a slow pace else you'll find that the wind had fun too, whistling through your veil and hairstyle and leaving it looking like it was hit by a hurricane.

Current Trends: Headons Wedding Service, 25, Hill Street, Dublin 1, Ph 8746289, have vintage limousines, landaus and broughams.

I asked Wayne Headon about the disadvantages of the open carriage on a wet day. "No problem," he assured me. "We'd ring the bride on the morning of the wedding. If a landau has been booked she can either change to a a brougham, so she still has a horse drawn carriage. If the weather is really bad we can supply a limo. We find that having decided on a horse-drawn carriage, most brides are very reluctant to change. The maximum trip for the landau is twenty-four miles. If the bride and groom live near the church, I'll collect the groom, the bridesmaids, the bride and her father and then take the couple to the reception venue. The carriages come in three colours, ivory, yellow and black, and red and black. On the morning of the wedding I decorate the landau with fresh flowers and ribbons to match the bridal party. It costs around £130 for one horse and £260 for two horses. Our service is nationwide. We are fully insured although by law you don't need to be insured to drive a horse and carriage, we just prefer to be. Our vintage car costs £100, our limousines £75."

Transporting the Guests

Increasingly, especially with the crackdown on drinking and driving, many couples are providing transport for guests who wish to avail of it, in the form of buses. Since the service was set up three years ago, the white Dublin Bus has gone from one to eight buses. In the morning the white bus is bedecked with flowers and the music of your choice is played for your guests. A green bus does the last trip. This service, confined to a radius of ten miles outside of Dublin, costs £160 and includes three trips. The morning trip, starting at the church after the ceremony, takes the guests to the reception venue. The evening trip takes the after-dinner guests from a designated pick-up stop to the reception venue. The last trip takes a designated route, dropping people as near as possible to their homes. For an extra £20 the bride can be brought to church by bus no doubt with the tape playing *Get me to the Church on Time*.

Dublin Bus, 59 Upper O'Connell Street, Ph 8720000, Ext 3060.

The Wedding Car Checklist

✍ Name, address, phone:

✍ Contact:

✍ Chauffeur:

✍ Footman:

✍ Colour/make of car:

✍ Extras ordered, TV, phone, champagne:

✍ Horse-drawn carriage, number of horses:

✍ Vintage car/make/open/hooded:

✍ Will transport be decorated:

✍ Colours agreed:

✍ What time will groom be collected:

✍ What time will bridesmaids be collected:

✍ What time will bride/father be collected:

✍ Price agreed:

MAKING MUSIC

❦

"If music be the food of love, play on;
Give me excess of it."
Twelfth Night Shakespeare

It's extraordinary how one snatch of a bar of music can linger in the memory and evoke the moment long after it occured.

I am absolutely certain that Wagner's Bridal March, *Here Comes the Bride*, was composed to draw tears from a stone. Hackneyed though it be, it turns my tap on every time I hear it.

The music you pick for your wedding is an important expression of your personality; be careful choosing it. Music is often chosen hastily on the recommendation of others, or as I did myself with unfortunate results. What passes for music to others may sound like mayhem to you. There is only one way to choose the music for your wedding—with your ears. Take the time to listen, listen and listen. Go to the church and listen to the resident organist playing. Does it please you or is it a right old din? Do the same with the soloist, before engaging his/her services. Don't engage anyone without hearing them, in situ if possible. Listen to their line of banter. Is that what you want? Always make the choice with your ears because if on the day you don't like what you have chosen, it's your ears that will hurt the most.

Spend time in the record library where the librarian will be able to offer plenty of suggestions. This task pays double dividends. If you make it so, this task offers a pleasant distraction from the hustle and bustle of shopping and running around before the wedding

Marry with Taste

and then it pays musical dividends on the day. The library in the Ilac Centre in Henry Street, with its huge collection of opera and classical music, has particularly good pickings.

Many of the the large record stores around the country have listening booths where you can listen to CDs on request. If not, go in at a quiet time and ask for the pieces to be played on tape or CD.

The most impressive music I ever heard at a wedding was provided by a string quartet. Even the wooden instruments had a visual dignified presence and the sound, so gentle when compared to the usual organ music, blended in perfectly with what was a very quiet, oak panelled, sunlit chapel.

Like most other aspects of the wedding plan, the scale of the church should be taken into account for your musical selection. Music sets the mood because it envelopes everyone simultaneously. People look at the dress, or at the flowers or at the cake at different times, but everyone listens to the music together.

For the church, the regular thing is to hire the soloist of your choice. If for any reason you also want, engage the organist of your choice, instead of using the resident organist, you may be asked to pay the fee of the resident organist too.

At the Church

In the anticipatory period before the wedding starts, the music should be subdued and solemn. A rousing tone, or the pealing of bells, announces the arrival of the bride.

Processional Music

The music for the walk up the aisle should be timed so that the bride can proceed at an unhurried regal pace. The music must end just as the bride reaches the altar.

In a church with a very long aisle, if the organist cannot see the bride, it's a good idea to give someone the duty to stay beside the organist to tell when the bride is within say ten rows of the altar. Otherwise if some delay occurs between the door and the altar, the bride may find herself approaching the aisle in an eerie deafening silence!

During the ceremony you can have a mixture of hymns, anthems, and increasingly selected secular pieces (check with the minister on these) sung by the soloist or choir.

Music during the Signing of the Register

This twenty-minute interval can be availed of by the organist to take flight in the metaphorical musical sense or for the choir to give full rein to its most rousing numbers. I don't think it's a good idea to ask the soloist to sing during the signing of the register. No matter how small the church, people will inevitably chat away regardless of the magnificence of the music. If you are going to have music have something that will either drown out or deter the chatterers.

Recessional Music

This calls for a jubilant, triumphant march, heralding the couple as they take their first, hopefully not faltering, steps together, down the aisle, as man and wife.

The Pealing Bells

Nowadays, the bells don't ring out very often for anyone or his gal. If you're getting married in a church with a good bell-ringing tradition its worth checking to see if you can have bell-ringers on your day. It's one of the most traditional and thunderingly triumphant ways of announcing the tremendous news to the neighbourhood at large. The priest or minister in charge will know the bell-ringers.

Reception Music

If the music you pick for the church reflects your joint personalities, what you choose for the reception should take into account that your guests probably range in age from seven to seventy. There should be something for everyone. Whether you hire a band or disc jockey, since you pay the piper, you pick the tunes. Traditionally, the bride and groom lead the dancing. If you have a particular song with symbolic associations ask the band to learn it, if necessary, and set the ball rolling with it. These arrangements should be made when booking the band, especially set the volume decibels that you want. Some disco systems seem to start at screaming pitch and end at hysteria.

The music should facilitate the dancers without reducing those seated to a state of mute silence. Remember, the Irish are a nation of talkers who sometimes dance, not vice versa. Traditional Irish music is a very safe bet and recently a lot of traditional bands, even those who sing "as gaeilge," have incorporated rock into the music, it's a dynamic combination. Make sure the band can play a variety of music. Alternate waltzing, jiving, rock and modern music. Set dancing has taken the country by storm in the past five years, even if only a handful of people know the steps, for the rest to follow can be great craic. Allow time for a family sing-song either before the band arrives or after their departure.

Music for the Bride's Arrival

Handel	Arrival of the Queen of Sheba
Handel	Minuet from the Royal Fireworks
Handel	Water Music

Mozart	The Marriage of Figaro
Wagner	Bridal March from the opera Lohengrin—Here Comes The Bride
Clarke's	Trumpet Voluntaire
Purcell's	Trumpet Tune and Air
Verdi	Grand March from the opera, Aida

Hymns and Secular Songs for the Ceremony

(Check non-liturgical music not permitted in the Catholic Church.)

The Lord is my Shepherd, Psalm 23
Handel's Hallelujah—if you have a mighty choir
Ag Chríost an Síol
Gounod's Ave Maria
Praise my Soul the King of Heaven

Signing the Register

Bach	Jesu Joy of Man's Desiring for organ, choir or soloist
Mozart	Laudate Dominum

Recessional Music

Widor's	Toccata
Mendelssohn's	Wedding March from, A Midsummer Night's Dream,
Pachelbel's	Toccata in C

Music and the Celebration of Marriage is a comprehensive pamphlet, issued under the imprimatur of the Archdiocese of Dublin, which has a wide range of suggestions of suitable church music, including Irish music and the Sean O'Riada masses, *Aifreann I, Aifreann II*.

It ends with a list of non-liturgical numbers which

are often requested, obviously for sentimental reasons, but which are considered unsuitable for church celebrations.

The list includes:

All of me
Annie's Song
From a Distance
Hawaiian Wedding Song
Help me Make it through the Night
I don't Know how to Love him—from Jesus Christ Superstar
I'll Walk with God (!)
In a country churchyard
I only Have Eyes for you
Lady in Red
Let it be
Norwegian Wood
Oh Grace
This is my Lovely Day
The Wedding
When you Wish upon a Star
When I'm 64
When I need you
Yesterday
You needed me

Setting Trends

Singer Maura O'Connell had no qualms about mixing her musical metaphors for her own wedding in April 1993.

Before her arrival, her guests inside Ennis Pro-Cathedral were entertained by a string quartet. Her arrival at the Pro-Cathedral was heralded by uileann piper, Kevin Murray, who played until she and her father reached the door of the church.

Once inside, Clarke's *Trumpet Voluntaire* was sounded and accompanied the procession up the aisle.

Local soloist Maretta O'Hehir sang Schubert's *Ave Maria* and *Panis Angelicus* while the American soul singer, Claudia Masser, sang a gospel hymn.

That's entertainment.

All-Irish weddings are much in demand in recent years, usually, though not always, accompanied by traditional Irish music.

Irish Music

Ag an bposadh a bhí i gCana
Bí Iosa im chroise
Grá mo chroí
Is maith an bhean Mhuire mhór
A Iosa bhain
A Rí an Domhnaigh
Ag Críost an Síol
Sé an Tiarna m'Aoire
Molaigí an Tiarna
Fion agus Uisce

Music Checklist

✍ ORGANIST
Name, address, phone:

Fee agreed:

Music chosen:

Date for practise:

✍ BELLRINGERS
Name, address and phone of leader:

Fee agreed:

✍ SOLOIST
Name, address, phone:

Fee agreed:

Music chosen—1, 2, 3:

Date for practise:

✍ CHOIR
Name, address and phone of leader:

Fee agreed:

Music chosen—1, 2, 3:

Date for practise:

🎵 MUSIC FOR RECEPTION
Name, address and phone of band leader/disc jockey:

Fee agreed:

Time to arrive/leave:

Music chosen:

Interval agreed:

BUYING THE PHOTOGRAPHY

❦

> "Next time I have the happiness to see you, I am determined to paint another portrait of you from life, in my best manner, for memory will not do in such minute operations."
> William Blake, 11th September 1801

Since the advent of the video, photography has lost its preciousness, the photograph as the sole chronicler of the all important day is no longer valid. Perhaps because of that sea change, photography is changing too, responding to new demands.

That is not to say that wedding photography is not precious. It is. That's why it must be chosen with such care. It's something that cannot be replaced if found unsuitable.

In America they have a one hundred per cent way of ensuring that your wedding photographs are perfect, they shoot them two weeks before the wedding! It's a bit presumptuous and being America should result in some very interesting court cases should the wedding be cancelled. But you have to admit, knowing the pictures are in the can before the wedding could be a real comfort, especially for the nervous bride and groom.

Another American idea that has crept into Ireland in recent times is the pre-wedding photograph. This is a formal engagement photograph which is enlarged and hung in the foyer of the reception venue on the day of the wedding for the guests to ogle at as they file in to be fed. To me that says, look at me and look at me again. Ugh.

A number of couples I talked to remarked that they

found the photographer an intrusive presence on their day. They felt they had to perform for the camera instead of the camera performing for them. One nurse, who admitted she hated getting her photograph taken at any time, said she only began to enjoy her day when the photographer left and he was a personal friend as well as a professional. Not surprisingly she didn't like the pictures when they arrived!

Practise being Photographed!

While the American "before" idea seems a bit far fetched, there is a lesson to learn from it. If you are not used to having your photograph taken, it might be a worthwhile exercise to get a friend to take a few rolls of film of you and your intended long before the wedding.

Examine the results. If there is something you don't like about yourselves try to either change it or mask it on your wedding day.

A missing tooth should never be revealed. Is one profile better than the other? How do your hands and nails look in the photographs? Should you wear gloves or grow your nails? A photograph will show you things you never see in the mirror.

Bear in mind that if you choose a friend to do the photography and then don't like the result, you may suffer the loss of a valuable friendship as well as the loss of the photographs.

I don't know if it's possible to find a photographer who will allow you to buy the negatives. Photographers hold on to negatives for obvious commercial reasons but when you think of it, it only makes sense for the subject of the photographs to have the negatives than for the mere executioner of the photograph.

A couple I know whose house was unfortunately gutted to the ground only minutes after they left it to go to Mass wanted to get another wedding album to have for their children. But the photographer was dead and the negatives gone.

Colour versus Back and White

Photography has indeed gone back to the future! Although colour is still predominantly used for wedding photographs, if you want to be up there with the arty set, then the trend is for black and white and sepia photographs.

They are considered the haute couture of photography. Photographers report that many couples are opening the album with two facing black and white pictures and the rest in colour. But as with the wedding dress, don't choose black and white because its fashionable, if you want full technicolour, get it.

Formal or Informal?

The posed picture is fast becoming very non-U. The picture with the two heads in the chalice or on the ceiling of the church or peeping through the keyhole, are seen as fantasy shots with absolutely nothing to do with what happened on the day.

In circles where photography is regarded as an art rather than a trade these pictures are condemned as being in bad taste and the photographers who take them are regarded as practitioners of bad taste.

Document your Day

What your wedding album should be is a document of the day as it occurred, not as a manipulating photographer decided it should be.

The pictures should capture the nervous excitement of the morning, the solemnity of the church service, and the jollity of the family relaxing afterwards.

To do that, the photographer must blend in with the

proceedings, catch the exclusive unrehearsed moment as it occurs and freeze it forever. He/she must not stuff a flash-gun into your face just as you deliver the most important two words of your life, "I do."

Tell the photographer exactly what you do and don't want. The photography you buy should respond to you and not you to it. The day should be documented in such a way that it is allowed to unfold naturally so that you can relive it again every time you look at the pictures.

Of course, if you really want the traditional posed shots, by all means have them, or you could get a combination of formal and candid pictures.

Choosing the Photographer

Try to see as many recent wedding albums as possible. Go to your own local church and watch wedding photographers at work. Is there anything happening that you do or do not like? Make a note of it. Once you have decided on a photographer you'll need to put down a booking deposit, perhaps as far as one year ahead for a summer Saturday booking.

If you don't know a photographer, there's an Association of Wedding Photographers listed in the Golden Pages.

It's important to hire a wedding photographer, they're used to getting crowds to do what they want them to do, in a most charming manner of course, in the shortest space of time.

What Makes a Good Photograph

1. Clarity and focus. Are the images clear? Are the edges sharp?
2. Is the lighting right? Are the faces well-lit and unshadowed?
3. Are the informal shots special moments or simply

awkward moves that might have been best unrecorded?

4. Is there anything intruding where it should not? In one of my wedding photographs, there's an orange lampshade above my head that looks like a witches' hat.

5. Is the group taken from an interesting angle or just lined up behind each other like the communist parties of old?

6. Watch out for the leaning Tower of Pisa syndrome. Are the pictures framed correctly or are some of the lines tilting?

Getting Permission

Some churches, Protestant more than Catholic, forbid the taking of photographs inside the church during the ceremony. Before the wedding, the photographer should talk to the minister to find out exactly what is permissible. Advance communication can save a lot of misunderstanding.

Price: The starting price for wedding albums is about £400 for twenty, 10 x 8 inch photographs. For this price the photographer begins at the church and ends at the reception.

For an extra charge of £75, the photographer will go to the family home one hour before the wedding. (I would have thought that mandatory rather than optional!) This means you now need to buy thirty pictures not twenty, so the album is £500. An Our Son's/Our Daughter's wedding album, with twelve, 7 x 5 inch photographs, will cost about £150 each. Total £900.

It's not cheap but it's something that will last a lifetime, that's why the photographer must be chosen carefully, not by word of mouth but on photographic evidence.

Not surprisingly, award-winning photographers like to

advertise their achievements in the Golden Pages etc. This puts them in demand and ups their price. That's consumerism. Get a written guarantee that, barring a fatality, the photographer you've booked will be the photographer who takes the shots and not a right hand man or woman. If that happens, sue, even if the pictures are perfect, it's the principle that's wrong.

Photographers who take pictures of guests often leave it to the bride to sort out payment and delivery of these prints. What that means is, the bride ends up working for the photographer and not the other way around.

Tell the photographer in advance that if he takes pictures of your guests, the contract is between them, you want to know nothing!

Having said that, my favourite picture of myself and my husband is one we had taken at a wedding when I, much to my mother's distress, was bridesmaid for the third time. She, of course, thought that ruled out my ever being a bride.

Photography Checklist

- Name address and phone of photographer:

- Has a named photographer been guaranteed:

- Contact:

- Deposit paid:

- Amount to be paid prior to wedding:

- Balance due:

- Who will hang the pre-wedding photo in the hotel foyer:

- What time is photographer due at bride's home:

- What time due at church:

- Has permission for church shots been requested:

- Granted:

- Has stop-over in rose garden been arranged:

- Album ordered:

- How many photos:

- Matt or glossy:

- ✎ No. of special effects photographs agreed:

- ✎ Black and white:

- ✎ Colour:

- ✎ Sepia:

- ✎ Price of album for parents:

- ✎ When will proofs be ready:

- ✎ How long can we have proofs:

- ✎ How long after choosing from proofs will album take:

THE VIDEO

"When you are old and grey and full of sleep,
and nodding by the fire."

WB Yeats.

Isn't that what a wedding video is all about? Capturing a precious experience and keeping it as a place to be revisited all the days of our lives.

"It's like a haze. We hardly remember anything, except that we enjoyed it." How many bridal couples have uttered the same sentiments about the most important day in their life!

Which is what makes the video such a huge attraction. In the euphoria of the day, many intimate moments occur, most of which the bride and groom cannot share in, unless it is a very small intimate wedding.

Before he became the proprietor of the 101 Restaurant in Talbot Street, Pascal Bradley spent years as a video operator, doing the weddings of the famous and the not-so-famous. His advice is straightforward and simple:

"Pick a professional, because once the day is gone you cannot recapture it. OK, some members of the family could dress up again in their wedding suits and some of the shots could be re-enacted but while that can work for photographs, the video is a different product altogether. A good video captures the essential atmosphere of a wedding, not just the mug shots.

"If you don't know a video operator pick a few names from the Golden Pages, members of the Professional Videographers Association. If they have a decent-sized office and a reasonable amount of equipment, then you can take it they are in the business for the long haul. If they are working from home with a business card, while they might be brilliant, the chances are they're starting out, fine for parties, but not your wedding day, you want the best.

"Phone three companies. Write down what each is offering for how much. Call into each. They'll probably show you their show reel. Know that the show reel is often shot on broadcasting tape and then edited for hours. The video you'll get may be on ordinary video, unedited. Having watched the show reel, ask to see a video of their most recent wedding, because that's their average production and it will be more comparable to what they'll do for you than the show reel. Check that the operator has a back-up video in case of an emergency."

Hot Tip: A good video operator is like a fly on the wall, you shouldn't be aware of their presence. Unlike the photographer who'll demand at least one and a half hours of your time, after the wedding ceremony and before the meal, the video operator should remain on the outside of the group and not go around jamming his video up the noses of the guests.

"On the altar, for instance, the video operator can be hidden behind pillars with a zoom lens and the video mounted on a tripod. Close-ups are not a problem, provided the photographer is at a discreet distance.

"Every video operator has their own lore of video stories. I once had a bride who was totally uncooperative. She didn't want a wedding video, but yielded to pressure from her mother who hired me. It was awkward.

"Happily, she was delighted with the video afterwards. Another bride was totally cooperative, in fact, too cooperative. She swished her skirt to show her bridal garter, but her uncle, a reverend gentleman, was not too pleased when her beautiful bum came up on the screen. Needless to say, I got the task of editing it out. Another couple I videoed signing the register had me edit that too for some mysterious reason! I ask no questions.

"The love-child, born to the couple before the big day, is often a problem. Of course, such matters are becoming increasingly more relaxed these days.

"Indeed, some couples flaunt the love-child, dress it up as an attendant and make it the centrepiece. Others will try, not so much to hide the child, as to keep it discreetly at bay and while no one actually tells you to exclude the child, you know instinctively that's what they want.

"The new trend is to include, at the beginning of the video, are photographs of the couple when they were children, teenagers, young adults, sort of leading up to the big event feeling."

Hot Tip: Plan exactly what shots you want and don't want. Usually the video begins at the bride's house, before she leaves for the wedding. No rollers please. Then its back to the church for the guests arriving, then to the hotel for the speeches and the first dance. Unlike the amateur who'll take hours of footage to be sure to get some good shots, the professional video operator should have little to edit, just a layer of music to add.

Pascal's business partner, Dick Conroy, from Celebration Video, 1 Beresford Place, Dublin 1, Ph 8742388, adds:

"No video should be longer than one and a half hours. Remember *The Godfather* only lasts two hours with a shooting every three minutes and even that runs out of steam. Everybody at the wedding should be videoed. Obviously a video of the bride at the house and church will cost less than a video which also includes the reception, it's the difference between two and eight hours. Church-only videos start at £150, while a church and reception video can cost £300—£700. The original copy goes to the bride and groom because that is always the best. Extra copies cost about £30, while the transfer fee to make the copies suitable for the American system is £30."

Video Checklist

- Name, address, phone:

- Contact:

- Agreed fee:

- Copies fee:

- Transfer fee for America:

- Agreed shots:

- Has permission for the video inside church been granted:

- Has lighting been checked:

- Will music be layered on:

- Is copyright fee agreed and paid:

- What time will the video operator arrive at bride's house:

- Date for delivery of video:

THE RECEPTION

🌿

"The charm dissolves: th' aerial music's past,
The banquet ceases, and the vision flies."
William Shenstone, 1764

Finding the Venue

Your wedding reception can cost from zilch to zillions depending on the venue and the menu. The determining factor is money. Count it. See how much you have. Since it's a "vision that flies," don't borrow for it. There was a time when a lavish wedding reception spelt social mobility, now it's more like to be seen as stupidity, with guests conspiratorially discussing the source of your revenue. Making savings makes sense in today's strapped times. Waste is frowned upon.

That said, the hotel reception is the number one choice for the majority of couples for the very good reason, though it is not cheap, it's easy to organise, is flexible, and very reliable.

A glance in the Golden Pages and you'll see, nationwide, the mid-week wedding can avail of great savings. As well as reduced prices on the menus, up to £5/£7 per head off the weekend charge, some hotels offer free bridal limousine service, a saving of £100—£160. Free bridal suites, free floral decorations, free tea/coffee/sherry reception plus free red/white wine with the meal or free sparkling wine toast.

Mid-week is often dismissed because people have to take a day off work for the wedding and then go to work tired the next day. But if you have a four o'clock wedding, the guests' day off could run from lunchtime of the wedding day to the lunchtime of the next day, thereby leaving a few extra hours to recover.

Comparing Like with Like

Some hotels boast that they cater for only one wedding per day. That's no proof that your reception will be any better there, than in a hotel with more than one reception.

Hotels doing more than one wedding per day go to great lengths to keep the wedding parties separated so that the brides are not bumping into each other and looking two a penny.

If the hotel reception is your first preference, check out at least ten hotels, meet the banqueting managers, get the full price details in writing. Look at the reception room, bridal suite, limousine and everything else on offer.

If you are getting free sparkling wine or a free sherry reception look at the labels and make a note of them.

Sampling and Simulating

Sample the food, access the service, know exactly what's on offer. Hotels differ in standards of hygiene and luxury. Some make a virtue of having toilet paper in the loo, others pamper patrons as a matter of policy.

The Cost

What you want is the hotel that will attend your guests at a price you can afford. £2,000 is the average cost for one hundred people in a hotel. You can invite another hundred to the evening reception for a mere £100, that's £1 per head for finger sandwiches. Menu-wise, the flexibility of the hotel depends on how eagerly they want to cater for your wedding. I asked Frank Rodgers of the Burlington Hotel, Upper Leeson Street, Dublin 4, Ph 6605222, if it would be possible to eschew their normal menu and have a soup/sandwiches and dessert reception instead.

He said, "No. I don't think we'd be too keen on such an idea because we feel it could have a negative affect on the Burlington Hotel. When you tell someone you were at a wedding, the first question they nearly always ask is what was the food like. If you tell them soup and sandwiches, they're not going to be impressed and they won't always think, well that's what was ordered. Rather will they think, I'm surprised at that for the Burlington! We prefer patrons to select from tried and trusted menus which we know people enjoy."

Booking the Venue

When you have decided on the hotel, book it. In Dublin there are plenty of choices but in the west of Ireland hotels can be booked as far ahead as two years for a Saturday wedding. I know a couple who considered themselves lucky to get a cancellation at Hayden's of Ballinasloe, eighteen months before their wedding.

The Marquee

After the hotel, the marquee is the second most popular choice of venue for Irish weddings. The marquee has been streamlined. The ropes and poles that used to shake and threaten havoc if someone sneezed have been replaced with free-standing, sturdy units; they go up and come down easier, can be decorated with designer-style interiors to match the theme of your wedding. There is no time-limit on the festivities, it can be cheaper to sit everyone in one go rather than have the main and after double up. They also come with lighting, heating, lining, tables, chairs and toilets. On the latter point, Adrian and Jackie Shine (whose medieval wedding reception was held in a marquee), cited the toilet facilities as the one aspect they disliked about their marquee wedding.

You set the location for the marquee, the beach, the wood, the local green, nice, if you want to go on a sentimental setting trip, perhaps to the very spot where you met. Ah!

Price

For £900 + 12 1/2 % VAT you'll get a 40' x 30' marquee, supplied, erected and removed, to seat one hundred people. That would include ruched roof linings, ruched wall linings from a choice of colours, carpeted flooring with a wooden dance area and lighting.

Cost of Furnishings and Food

Add £350 for ten tables and one hundred chairs and £1,000 (if the caterer comes in at £10 a head), that's over £2,000 for the marquee and food alone, the same price as the hotel which can accommodate a morning and evening reception for two hundred people. The decision to hire a marquee is obviously not motivated by money. It's really a matter of deciding which venue offers the things you most want. The marquee's trump card is that it offers privacy and flexibility of location. If you're torn between whether to have a hotel or marquee reception write out the advantages and disadvantages which each venue has for your particular style of wedding.

The Family Home

Don't overlook the family home if numbers are small. It's normally decked out at it's best at the time of a wedding anyway. It too offers privacy, and you could bring in outside caterers. You can still organise an evening reception, either on your wedding day, or as is increasingly happening, after the honeymoon.

TREASA BROGAN

To Buy Or Not To Buy—Alcohol

Wine comes in at the mouth
And love comes in at the eye;
That's all we shall know for truth
Before we grow old and die.
I lift the glass to my mouth,
I look at you, and I sigh.
   A Drinking Song, WB Yeats

In Ireland, drink presents a particular problem, which is cultural as well as economic. People often worry that if they don't ply their guests legless they'll be regarded as skinflints. Not so. When Brendan Grace advises the father of the bride to buy no drink, then you know the times are changing.

True story. A publican I know who has been in the business for over thirty years, offered to buy the drink at his son's wedding. Knowing the number of wedding guests, he set aside what he considered would be the cost. He was staggered by the bill and by the fact that it took him by surprise. He thought he knew everything about the drinking habits of the Irish.

Mary Kerrigan is the Bar Banqueting Manager at the Burlington Hotel. I asked her had she noticed any changes in the drinking habits of wedding parties in recent years:

"Yes. Up to 1991 most weddings had an open bar, when the host took the tab at the end of the night. That has gone almost entirely. Most couples buy the wine for the meal and the toast, sparkling champagne or a round of drinks, leaving the guests to buy their own drink after that. Yes, you can see a huge increase in the amount of alcohol consumed when the bar is open, as against the amount of drink consumed when people are paying for it themselves."

The Reception Checklist

- ✍ Name, address, phone:

- ✍ Contact:

- ✍ Approximate numbers agreed:

- ✍ Menu agreed:

- ✍ To include wine:

- ✍ Toast:

- ✍ Price per head including drink:

- ✍ Who sets the place cards:

- ✍ When can everything be checked before wedding:

- ✍ Do we want licence extension:

- ✍ Is there a car parking facility for each guest:

- ✍ If the meal is buffet is there table room and a seat for each guest:

- ✍ How many people will serve the main meal:

- ✍ Is there a room for the bride and groom to change in:

- Caterers for marquee reception:
- Menu agreed:
- Number agreed:
- To be served at what time:
- Is wine/toast included:
- Caterer to supply tables and chairs:
- Number of tables and chairs agreed:
- Price agreed:
- Marquee supplier:
- Price agreed:
- Marquee to be set up on:
- Marquee to be removed:
- Flooring:
- Toilet facilities:

MARRY ON A BUDGET

❦

"Here's to the maiden of bashful fifteen
Here's to the widow of fifty
Here's to the flaunting, extravagant queen;
And here's to the housewife that's thrifty."
School for Scandal, RB Sheridan, 1777

Guy de Maupassant's wonderful short story, *The Necklace*, has a telling lesson for those who would be thrifty and marry on a budget. *The Necklace* is about a woman who borrows and loses the necklace of a very rich friend. She sells her house and spends decades scrubbing floors to repay the loan she took out to replace the necklace.

Twenty-five years pass before she meets the owner of the necklace. She breaks down and confesses all. If you have ever read Maupassant you've guessed the end. Yes, the original necklace was a fake. There are two ways to marry on a budget. One is to fake it, hide it, cover it up, pretend you're loaded. The other is to flaunt it.

The first approach, being furtive, breeds resentment, and leaves people jumping to wrong conclusions.

The second evokes sympathy. Not only do people not waste your money, they'll join you in thinking up cost-cutting ways to save it. It becomes a campaign and you're the winner.

Remember any idiot can Marry with Taste—with money. But it sure takes intelligence and flair to Marry with Taste—without money. It's a challenge that needs oceans of imagination and a relentlessly confident determination to carry it off. Be warned, it's time consuming, ergo, the more time you give it, the more money you'll save. But, happily, it's not only fashionable, it's very Pee Cee.

As with the monied wedding, you must prioritise, plan and pray!

Before you marry on a budget learn how to get what you want, at a price you can afford.

If you follow a few simple rules, success will be yours in abundance.

I make no apology for the fact that I buy second-hand. I used to be secretive about it, slightly ashamed. Then I saw superstar, Jeremy Irons, on the Late Late Show with his wife, Sinéad Cusack. When he described his favourite form of relaxation as scouring the rubbish heaps of Paris for treasure, I recognised a soul-mate. Now if Hollywood stars go rooting around in rubbish tips and flea markets, isn't it THE in-thing to do?

Of course it is, you gotta believe it!

One month before my wedding day, quite by chance, I hit upon a way to buy second-hand which has served me well ever since. I forget why, but we needed or wanted to buy the Encyclopaedia Britannica, but we hadn't got the money. We watched the advertisement sections of many newspapers but no EB appeared. We decided to try a Wanted Encyclopaedia Britannica advertisement in the *Evening Press*. Well, it was like unloosing a flood gate. They came at us, from miles away, with dog-eared dusty volumes that went back three decades. Eventually we hit gold when we were offered a brand new, deluxe, gilt-edged set. The man selling the books had no interest in them. They were still boxed. He told us he nearly puked when he was presented with them as a retirement present. We got them for half the going price and left him smiling.

Wanted advertisements have specific advantages over For Sale advertisements.

I ended up living on Cypress Grove Road, Dublin 6, because I advertised for a house on Cypress Grove Road, when what I wanted was a house *off* Cypress

Marry with Taste

Grove Road!

Rule One: If you are specific about what you want the chances are you'll get it.

Example: Wanted designer wedding dress, size 12, white lace, long, sheath shape, preferably Paul Costello.

You may think that's a long shot, but by being specific, you are also discouraging (never totally) the person with the size 16, mini-skirted, balloon dress from answering your advertisement.

Another advantage of the Wanted over the For Sale advertisement, is that the For Sale one attracts many buyers and the item goes to the highest bidder which puts the price up.

If the item is priced in the paper, it's sold to the first caller with money. When you call, as arranged, perhaps after a one hour drive, there it is, gone, as they say in Dublin.

It may not have been, but you always feel you missed a great bargain.

This doesn't happen with the Wanted advertisement. When you put your advertisement in the paper, it may seem obvious to say so, but you are the only customer for that item.

Some people would simply not advertise their goods for sale because:
(a) They'd be afraid anyone would see what they had.
(b) They'd fear friends would wonder if they were broke because they were selling off the silver.
(c) They'd live in dread that a horde of gawkers would trail around their showhouse, leaving fingerprints on the polished surfaces and footprints on the carpet.

Such people will answer Wanted advertisements, for a number of reasons:
(a) A Wanted advertisement means a genuine buyer.
(b) It's a way to have an item removed without paying removal fees. For instance, if they wanted to buy a new fridge or dining-room suite, then it's handy to have someone else come and take the old one away.

On the other hand:

Rule Two: Don't be rushed into buying, its better to lose a bargain than buy a booby.

Rule Three: Never buy until you have called to each of your respondents. Some people can make rubbish sound like the find of the century, while others undervalue their possessions.

Don't be mislead by accents, addresses or occupations! The cardinal rule is: Examine each item before you buy it, the way you'll examine it when you get home. Upside down and inside out.

Don't be embarrassed. Ask for assistance to move and turn.

Do beware, if the seller tut, tuts. It means, as Hamlet said, "something is rotten in the State of Denmark."

If you've driven miles to see what turns out to be a heap of junk only suitable for the Late Late Antique Show, don't bother arguing. It wastes time. People often genuinely believe that their decrepit possessions have gained value with age. Best leave them with their illusions. If you stay and argue, they might end up convincing you to buy something you instinctively knew you didn't want.

Rule Four: Know the new price of the item you want, and then decide how much you are prepared to pay for it second-hand.

My explicit experience has been that Wanted ads are worth their weight in gold. I'm continually amazed at how little those columns are used in the paper. They seem to be the prerogative of second-hand book and antique dealers.

It costs absolutely nothing to place an advertisement in *Buy and Sell* magazine. So start off there. But don't ignore the national and local papers. Advertisements in the local papers cost less than in the national papers but serve a smaller audience and free papers are often not read. Bought papers are read, though I'm obviously not saying everyone reads the advertisement columns.

Marry with Taste

Unlike auctions, sales or markets, the Wanted way puts you in total control of the operation.

So, you start off by placing an advertisement in the paper or media of your choice for an engagement ring, wedding ring, bridesmaid's presents, dress, head-dress, bridesmaid's dress, silk floral bouquets, groom's clothes.

Buying the Ring Second-hand

The AA run a service whereby they check out the reliability and value of a car before someone buys it.

Copy that idea if you are not buying your rings from a reputable jeweller. Simply ask the owner to agree to meet you at the Assay Office—see under Propose, Engage, Announce it—and have the ring valued and dated. The same goes for a ring from an antique shop. Anyone in the family got a family heirloom? Buy it.

The Dresses

Very often, second-hand bridal shops only stock dresses. But through an advertisement you may get the whole rig out, dress, shoes, bag, head-dress, veil. If your luck really holds you may even get the bridesmaid's and children's dresses too.

Hire everything. It's not exactly cheap but it's a good way to get the dress you really want.

Make your dress. Obviously if you have never taken to needlework this is not the time to start. But if you have some experience, you could make a simple basic dress and transform it with buttons, bows, lace trims, sequins, beads.

Although I had done a dressmaking course with the Grafton Academy ten years previously, when my daughter was making her Holy Communion I did a refresher ten-week course and made the dress under expert guidance.

While hand sewing may be tedious (I sewed one hundred dropped pearls to the bottom of my debs dress) it's simple to do and almost idiot-proof. I mean, a decorative beading does not need precision positioning. Anyone to help?

Evoke the Jane Austen era. Light a turf fire and invite the craft-workers in the family to a joint sewing session, sitting around the table working as in the old Irish meitheal spirit. Play Carolan's Harp Concerto. Absolutely no food, no tea in the room, serve later.

Swap labour. Most families have a craft-worker who might be delighted to sew for you, if you offer to scrub floors, cut the grass, do the shopping or wash the windows.

Scour the sales at Christmas, especially for soiled garments which can be easily cleaned. Don't buy a torn garment unless you know it can be repaired, such as a ripped hem or seam. A tear off the seam is very tricky to mask or mend.

Bridesmaids' dresses often cost less, order one in white.

Restoring: If your mother's wedding dress was not given to the nuns or priests to make vestments with, it may be on top of the wardrobe wrapped in tissue. Try it on.

Lyk-nu Cleaners, 4 The Mall, Donnybrook, Dublin 4, Ph 2692609 (see also under Dressing The Bride). Lyk-nu were recently granted an American licence (it's only in America that you would need a licence) to restore wedding gowns, using a special anti-sugar process. Eoin Hodkinson tells me they have sent a number of delighted daughters up the aisle wearing their mother's restored wedding dress. That's what the continuum is all about.

Marry with Taste

The Head-dress

To me, nothing adorns the face quite as startlingly as a halo of fresh flowers. It has an utterly organic affect totally in tune with the environmentally-conscious era that we live in. It costs about half the price of the shop decoration and doesn't need a veil.

Skull caps covered in lace or the material of the dress are easy to make and very reasonable, as is the netting that can be attached.

A single silk rose will hold the veil effectively too, as will a velvet headband covered in pearls, sequins or wrapped around with ivy, fake or real.

The Veil

Is there one in the family? If so, it may need treatment to match the white in the dress. Or sew a lace edging on to both the dress and the veil to give an overall unity.

Shoes

Shoes are important. Don't be crippled on your wedding day. It'll show on your face and in the photographs. Resist buying cheap white sandals.

Dye a pair of used comfortable sandals or shoes. Transform the shoes by glueing or sewing on a lace bow or a bow of matching material. You'll get a suitable needle in a craft shop. Have old shoes covered—see under Accessories. Watch the end of summer sales when white shoes are often sold off.

Photographs

How many times have you looked at your sister/friend's wedding album? Probably never. The vast majority of couples look at the wedding album three times in the first year of marriage before consigning it to the top of the wardrobe or the bottom of a book case.

OK, if Great Aunt Bertha returns from Canada within two years of the wedding, you might show it to her if she still wants to see it having sat through ninety minutes of the video.

What is on show, often for a lifetime, long after the video too has been consigned to the top of the wardrobe, is one particular framed photo above the mantelpiece, on top of the telly, or hanging on the wall.

So when all is said and done, what you really need is one professional photo. Many couples visit a rose garden or the photographer's studio on route from the service to the reception venue. In fact, it has become such a custom you'll see from the car-hire section of this book that most of the car-hire companies quote this stop in their prices. Arrange one session with your favourite photographer, en route to the reception.

Alternatively, you could arrange for a photographer to come and take a photo of you when you come out of the church or at the reception venue and you could also get a group photo taken then too.

You are now assured of one/two good photos.

Next step is to show an inordinate interest in the family albums of your friends/family. They'll absolutely purr when you ask to see the holiday snapshots.

Never mind the location, or the shock at seeing your most prim and proper aunt topless in Benidorm, look at the composition and the clarity of the picture. Is the photo focused properly? Are any of the heads/hands/fingers/feet, cut off? Does it look like night when in fact it was day? Never assume that the amateur photographer with the biggest battery of equipment is the one who takes the best pictures.

If the chosen friend/relative is willing to oblige, you might very well decide that their wedding present is the taking and developing of the photographs. Discuss the

Marry with Taste

pictures you want and ask them to check the light in the service and venue location to see if indoor equipment is needed, especially for an evening wedding.

SAVE IT WITH FLOWERS

Grow Your Own!

If gardening is your hobby then why not save it with flowers? If it's not, don't even try, chances are you'll waste money and grow weeds. Is there an avid gardener in the family? Judging by the crowds in the garden centres there are hundreds. Depending on the season of your wedding you could ask him/her about the possibility of growing you roses/carnations/tulips/daffodils/wallflowers, perhaps as a wedding present or you could return a service in kind.

Beg

Foliage from relatives'/neighbours' gardens, especially the ubiquituous conifers. Add Gypsophilia and some single blooms for focus. This floristry is easily arranged in vases and containers.

At the Church: SHARE

Find out if there is another wedding booked for the same date as yours. If so, get in touch with the other couple to see if a neutral colour scheme can be agreed and costs shared.

Take Advantage of

Recently our local church resembled the Botanic Gardens, the sumptuous leavings of a high society wedding. Now if you had arranged to marry an hour or a day after such a wedding, well then you wouldn't do anything churlish, like asking for the flowers to be removed! Would you?

Sleuth out the dates and times of future weddings in your local church and book yours afterwards bearing in mind that they too might go for the Two-into-One Option, below.

The Church/Reception Venue

Two into One can go

Floral decorations for the church can run into hundreds, ditto for the reception. Arrange for someone discreet, not the joker in the pack, to take the flowers from the church to the reception venue and have them installed while the guests are having the pre-reception cup of tea/sherry. Even without a sherry reception, there will be plenty of time to shift the floristry from one venue to another.

However, I know that in some churches Saturday afternoon weddings are often asked to leave the flowers in place because it is too late for the regular florist to replace them. Have a chat with the minister marrying you.

You could agree to leave the church flowers on the altar and bring in your own free-standing arrangements as well. Or you could agree to leave some of your wedding flowers on the altar, in vases, and take the free standing arrangements to the venue.

Plants/Trees/Shrubs

Use potted flowers, plants, shrubs and trees. Trees still in their tub make a spectacular, short-term, indoor decoration. The plant pots can easily be masked with lace and ribbons, crêpe paper, or trailing ivy. Terracotta pots or planters painted to theme in with the bridal

Marry with Taste

party colour scheme, will add interest.

Very ornate pots, perhaps presents from the wedding gift list, could be given their first outing, watch the donor beam!

After the Wedding is Over

After the wedding you, or, (while you honeymoon!) the family gardener can take the potted plants, shrubs, flowers and trees home, and voila, your garden is set to grow.

Whatever about the bride and groom, the plants, the trees, and especially the potted daffodils, will go forth and multiply and, perhaps, be emblematic of those they served!

Very soon, or in the mists of time, you could hear yourself call, "Johnny, darling, come down here out of mummy and daddy's wedding tree."

Isn't that what marriage and the continuum is all about!

For the Bride

The simplicity of a floral head-dress, can be re-echoed in a basket of matching flowers and trailing ivy (cut from the garden wall the day before the wedding).

Baskets can be painted, but use ribbon on the handles.

Have a floral theme of single flower buds everywhere.

Cabbage roses make a demure statement sewn onto the rim of a straw hat.

Carry a sheaf of flowers.

Carry a posy of mix-dried and artificial flowers with real foliage or visa versa.

If you decide on a themed wedding, say yellow and white, give each guest a daffodil to wear before the ceremony.

The Guest/Gift List

Telling it by Telephone

A number of brides I talked to said they found when they sent out their wedding invitation, the invited one rang up and said thank you very much for the invitation, had a chat in general about the wedding and hung up without specifying whether or not they were going. In many cases these people subsequently sent no acceptance cards assuming the bride knew their intentions from the initial conversation. The brides then had to ring the invited ones again, in order to establish the number of affirming and refusing guests.

A much cheaper way to invite your guest is to set aside an evening, by day it's too dear, for the bride and the groom to ring the guests on her/his guest list. Allow three minutes per call.

Most people say 130 words in one minute. That's 400 words about ten times more than on an invitation card. Have your spiel written out before you start. Set the egg timer.

No. 1: "Hello. Is Mary there? Hello Mary. I'm inviting you and Sean to my wedding on Saturday, June 4th 1994 at three o'clock in the chapel in Trinity College. Fergal and myself hope you can come. You can. That's great."

No. 2: "Hello.... Check it out and let us know as soon as possible, we have to book the hotel early."

No. 3: "Hello.... Sorry you can't, I understand."

These three conversations take under one minute, allowing Mary thirty seconds to get to the phone. That leaves two minutes for chit-chat which should/could conclude with,

"By the way, did you know our gift list was with...."

Marry with Taste

Write to Invite

Write invitations, perhaps on pre-stamped postcards like the St Patrick's Day ones. They'd make a really apt invitation card for March 17th weddings.

Do a humourous computer print-out, with all of the details, not forgetting the gift list.

Hand deliver as many invitations as possible, or if the invitations are going out around Christmas, send them with the Christmas cards.

Keep an exact list of who has been invited.

Playful Place Cards

Every year my ten and twelve year old sons, Conor and Ciarán, make the to/from tags for the Christmas presents. They cut them using a special set of cardboard shapes, one of the shapes is a bell. Pay a small fee to engage the services of the budding artists in your family, usually over nine. Buy sheets of white cardboard. Get them to cut out as many heart or bell shapes as are necessary, with an extra amount just in case they are needed. Give the artists the name, occupations or hobbies of each guest and leave them to decorate each name appropriately. I guarantee those place cards will be a better conversation starter than the prettified shop variety.

Food and Drink

Unless you are addicted to cooking I'm positively against any bride going near any kitchen on her wedding day. Every survey across the western world testifies to the fact that women spend too much time in the kitchen, regardless of their professional status or that of their husband/partner.

Rule One: Not on your Wedding Day. Anyway if it's bad luck for a bride to taste her wedding cake before the wedding, it has to be bad luck for her to taste any of the food.

I know food and drink is where most couples find it hardest to cut back on their special day. After all, isn't a wedding meant to be a hooley? Aren't you supposed to eat, drink and be sick to prove it!

Things are changing. Sit down to any table nowadays and as the diners stuff their faces greedily, someone mentions the word diet and the entire table begins to moan in unison. Tomorrow, they all promise themselves.

The moral of the story is, the majority of the people who will attend your wedding will not be famished or undernourished. In fact, at least one-third of them will want to lose weight. The former won't want too much to eat, help the latter.

The Hotel Option

At present hotels cater for the majority of weddings. If there is a particular hotel you would like to have your reception in, why not decide on a reception budget and call in to the banqueting manager to see what is on offer for the number of guests you intend inviting. In these recessionary times, flexibility is the name of the game.

Hotels make more money on drink than on food. It might be possible for you to feed the troops and let them buy their own drink. Nowadays most people are happy to do that. It's the round system they dread. Ban it.

Local Hall

Recently I attended a self-service wedding, in a sports hall with the food provided by brought-in caterers. We had tea/sherry reception, seafood starter, a large barbecued steak, done on the patio outside the hall, jacket potatoes, a choice of side salads, a choice of fresh fruit salad and cream or black forest gateaux, tea/coffee. I don't think it was good because it cost £10 a head, it was good because the food was delicious.

Outside caterers are flexible, you design the menu to suit your pocket as well as your palate. Outside caterers also know which venues are good and which are grotty. Use their experience when making your choice.

The Pub around the Corner is not the Same

Because I can't drink (no head), I don't frequent pubs very often. I have to be honest and say that when I got an invitation to a small family affair wedding, with the reception in a pub, I sort of expected a soup and sandwiches spread and immediately thought of coordinating the denims.

Well, I couldn't have been more wrong. The ambience of the venue was palatial and the food was incredibly delicious. On enquiring, I found out that the chef had been snitched from a top class London hotel.

Ergo, the pub around the corner is not the same.

The wedding was in Madigans in Donnybrook, Ph 2830376, and on a warm Saturday in August 1993 we had it all to ourselves, barring a few patrons who eventually joined in the fun despite the rope. The pub has been recently refurbished and while it is on a par with the best of hotels for comfort, the price is remarkably good value. We picked from the carvery, a choice of four excellent starters, three main courses: lamb, beef and chicken. The bride's mother served the wedding cake with the tea/coffee and the cost was £7.95 per head. After the reception we were joined by 120 more guests whereupon we all headed upstairs to the Maisie Madigan Lounge where the nearest thing I've ever heard to an Irish rock band played Irish music and sang "as gaeilge." The *craic* and the *ceol* was mighty.

Mr Jimmy Byrne, the manager of Madigans tells me they can cater comfortably for up to 150 people in the upstairs lounge, which holds 270 people. The menu is negotiable; if you have x amount of money to be spent on y amount of guests, he will design a sandwich-free menu, unless of course, you definitely want sambos. Ask your local pub about providing food for your wedding party.

When you think of it, nearly every church in Ireland is within a spit of a pub. Set a new trend, walk from the church to your wedding reception.

Neighbours!

The more local your wedding, the more you can cut down on costs, because the more in control of the situation you are. You only have to get a puncture in Ireland to discover again what a generous nation of givers we are. Most people love being "in" on a wedding. For a small fee, neighbours and friends will be glad to help out for an hour or two. Give the ones who refuse the money a book token. Ask and you shall receive, said the Lord. Tap into the community spirit, I bet you'll be staggered at the generous response.

Instead of a main meal, serve soup, canapés, hors d'oeuvres, brown bread.

A sparkling wine for the toast is cheaper than champagne.

Have your local supermarket deliver cooked chickens, hams, cartons of coleslaw, corn, etc, to a hired room or sports hall on the day.

If it's a winter wedding, hire a room in a pub or hotel and serve hot mince pies, punch, and wedding cake.

TOASTS, TALKS AND THANK YOUS

"Speak the speech, I pray you, as I pronounced it to you, trippingly on the tongue; but if you mouth it, as many of your players do, I had as lief the town-crier spoke my lines. Nor do not saw the air too much with your hand, thus; but use all gently: for in the very torrent, tempest, and, whirlwind of passion, you must acquire and beget a temperance that may give it smoothness."
Hamlet, William Shakespeare

Hamlet's advice to the players is as relevant today as it was in Shakespeare's time.

You must be careful that what you say in a speech does not come back to haunt you. That's what happened to Viscount Althorpe, the brother of Princess Di and future Earl of Spencer, when he performed best man duties for his friend, Darius Guppy.

Darius Guppy personified what it is to be privileged. Of wealthy parents, his father is the explorer Nicholas Guppy, his mother the Iranian writer, Shusha. Darius grew up in the gilded bosom of the aristocratic classes. At Oxford, he took a double first in History and Languages. He is beguilingly handsome. When Darius married in 1992, the Viscount made a speech that was as witty as it was apocryphal. "I always knew," said the Viscount, "that Darius would either be a millionaire, or have visited the cells by the time he was thirty." Within weeks of that prophetic speech, and long before he was thirty, Darius was languishing in jail having been sentenced to five years imprisonment for his part in a one million pound insurance swindle.

I was at a wedding when the father of the bride sent

out a sour grapes signal to the groom and the groom's assorted relatives, me included. "Today I have lost a daughter, but gained a telephone." The sarcastic tone lacked joviality and the father lived to lose his telephone again, when his daughter returned home some years later.

Regardless of the speaker's vocal ability, speeches are very important. They can either send a cosy warm glow around the room or signal portentous times ahead. They are best when well planned and fully rehearsed, all the better for them to sound spontaneous.

The Bride's Father

Traditionally it falls to the bride's father to make the first speech. Bearing in mind that though brevity is the soul of wit, this speech will be forgiven if it is tenderly indulgent.

If daddy wants to take a trip down memory lane and recall, in detail, as Audrey's daddy did at a beautiful wedding I attended, all the charming milestones encountered from the time the little girl arrived into the world to the bridal banquet, then it is daddy's privilege to do that. Most people present will be delighted to go the course with him. If a wedding is not a time for poetry, love, nostalgia, emotion and happy tears, to be scattered like confetti, when is?

Brendan Grace's father of the bride speech, known both sides of the Atlantic Ocean, tickled Frank Sinatra pink when Brendan performed it for Frank in Dublin some years ago and resulted in Brendan being invited to do the warm-up for Frank in Wembley a few months later.

Watch it if you want to know what definitely not to do. I asked Brendan if he had any serious advice to offer to the aspiring father of the bride: "Well not having been in the position myself, I can only guess. First of all, the father of the bride should not pay for the toast. Too much money is wasted on drink. But he should have plenty of money in case he wants to buy drinks for people on an individual basis. But when you think of it, they should be treating him, yeah. At the meal, the bride and groom are usually first to be served. The father could think of handing out the cake to the top table, this would get him up and moving and might help him to loosen out before he begins to talk. I don't think I met one father who wasn't scared...sugarless...at the thought of giving a speech. The speech should be humourous. All about the courtship and the worrying and the having to get up at night and let the daughter in because she forgot her key and how sheepish the groom used to look, all that sort of thing.

"In one of my gags I say I'm losing a breadwinner and gaining a dependent, that's because my imagined daughter is a working girl until her unemployed boyfriend gets her up the pole. But seriously, always end on a sincere note," concluded Brendan.

If the bride's parents are dead, or not available, it usually falls to a brother, family friends, godfather or whoever gave the bride away, to do this honour, when how proud the parents would have been is inevitably mentioned.

Whoever makes it, the first speech ends with a toast "To the bride and groom."

The Groom's Speech

This follows that of his new father-in-law. It begins with a series of thank yous, especially to the in-laws, if they have provided the reception and ends with a toast to the bridesmaids and pages. It can be long or short depending on the personality of the groom, again the audience should be indulgent.

The Best Man's Speech

Undoubtedly, the wittiest speech of the day is expected of the best man! Here the chance to settle old scores must be resisted. Nor is it the time for something borrowed or something blue to be mentioned either. I heard a best man give a detailed summary of the groom's previous sexual exploits to the utter disenchantment of everyone, especially the groom. Wedding speeches, like the sparkling champagne, should be easy to swallow.

One of the best man's duties is to read out messages. In the days of the telegram, these were mercifully short. But with the arrival of the dreaded fax, long-winded friends and relatives can wax lyrical, in absentia. In bundles these faxes make for very boring listening. While the father of the bride is making his speech, the best man should sift through the messages, selecting the witty ones for inclusion and leaving the boring "very best wishes" ones to the end. However, a message from a very close relative abroad or in hospital, should be read first and in full.

The best man's speech has no formal toast but usually ends with another toast to the bride and groom.

The Bride Speaks!

Brides, like the lambs, have suffered centuries of silence. Not anymore. Today's bride likes to say her own thank yous and why not?

It is a good idea for the intending speakers to get together. They needn't divulge everything they are going to say, but it helps to map out speeches so that a whole lot of tedious over-lapping can be avoided.

Some Speech Topics

If people feel confident to tell jokes, that's good, but if

Marry with Taste

they don't they should resist the temptation, jokes need skilful timing or they bomb. George Bernard Shaw, famous for being a long-winded speaker and raconteur, was asked to say something about sex at a wedding, "It gives me great pleasure," he announced and sat down.

There is the famous story of the Welsh rugby player who, on finding his bride a virgin on their wedding night, returned her to her parents the following morning, saying, "If she's not good enough for the rest of the team, she's not good enough for me either."

Poetry, plays and literature are rich sources of philosophical inspiration, none better than Shakespeare.

Indeed, the father's speech could take as its premise, the Shakespearian sonnet at the beginning of the book, "Let me not to the marriage of true minds/Admit impediments," and then offer a few words of wisdom on how to overcome these impediments.

Golf is a good allegory with which to dole out dollops of philosophical wisdom.

The father might point out that life is like a game of golf, with fairways and rough patches and how you get out of the bunker determines whether you win or lose the very difficult prize that is matrimony.

Or perhaps the father could offer Benjamin Franklin's advice, given in 1750. "Keep your eyes wide open before marriage, and half shut afterwards."

The bride might give notice that she intends watching out for the Maxim Gorky Syndrome. The Russian playwright didn't think women got a good deal from marriage. He said, "When a woman gets married it's like jumping into a hole in the ice, in the middle of winter, you do it once and you remember it the rest of your days." The American poet Jean Kerr, said much the same thing. "Marrying a man is like buying something you've been admiring for a long time in the shop window. You may love it when you get it home, but it doesn't always go with everything else in the house."

Perhaps the groom is a gardener, amateur or professional. Don't gardeners see marriage as a pair of shears, so joined that they cannot be separated, often moving in opposite directions, yet always punishing everything that comes between? When it comes to marriage, Shakespeare had it both ways, having recommended it in the famous sonnet, in *Twelfth Night* he condemns it "Many a good hanging prevents a bad marriage."

Robert Louis Stevenson agreed. He believed that, "Marriage is like life in this—that it is a field of battle and not a bed of roses."

Despite approving of sex, George Bernard Shaw resisted marriage for decades but eventually decided to take the plunge, saying, "Marriage is popular because it combines the maximum of temptation with the maximum of opportunity."

You can end your speech by comparing wedlock to a padlock, and then deciding, no, it's not, rather is it a way of halving griefs, doubling joys and quadrupling expenses.

Hints for Delivering the Speech

Recently on the South Bank Show, Sir Anthony Hopkins, who won an Oscar for his part, Hannibal Lector, in *The Silence of the Lambs*, admitted to Melvyn Bragg that he reads aloud what his character has to say at least 200 (!) times.

Sir Winston Churchill used to rehearse his speeches in the bath. One day, quite in error, his valet, thinking Sir Winston had called him, entered the bathroom. He was hastily evicted. "I wasn't calling you," said the Sir, "I was addressing the House of Commons."

If both of these magnificent speakers felt the need to practise, practise, practise before making a speech, then

Marry with Taste

you can take it as read that so do the rest of us, barring the odd family Hamlet.

Golden Rules: Don't drink before you make your speech. Look at the Brendan Grace video and see why.

Be prepared. The balance between not knowing the speech by heart, and not reading it, is easily achieved. Write, preferably type out, the speech, practise it in the mirror, then on the day use single prompt words to jolt the memory.

Have water ready in case your throat gets dry.

Don't ask for applause if your story is less than riveting, move on.

Include a quotation or snatch of poem, choosing one as apt as possible.

End when you know they are begging for more.

GETTING MARRIED IN A CATHOLIC CHURCH

When the Bride and Groom are Catholic

I did what every bride who wants to marry in a Catholic church has to do; I went to my local parish priest, Fr Brendan Heffernan.

"It's always a joy to marry a couple. I see my role as a priest to make sure the couple enjoy their wedding ceremony and to prepare them to live happily ever afterwards, a tall order, but we do our best. I like to be at ease and familiar with the couple on their wedding day; that entails a number of meetings, usually four."

Fixing the Date

Six months notice is required if either of you is under eighteen years of age.

Three months notice is required of all other couples.

The Marriage Documentation

1. A new Baptismal Certificate is required from each partner. This is obtained from the church where they were baptised. The reason a new certificate is necessary is to prevent bigamy. When a person marries, the information is recorded beside their baptismal information.

2. Confirmation Certificate from the church in which you were each confirmed.

3. Letter of Freedom is required from each parish, Tipperary, Toronto, etc, in which you lived for more than six months since you were sixteen years of age.

Your priest will help get these. The bride's papers are completed by her local priest. Ditto the groom.

Minors in civil law require the consent of parents/guardians.

The Ceremony

It's your day and you are allowed to shape it. You can ply your troth with a number of different texts, some longer than others. The groom can speak first or the bride can speak first.

You choose the readings from Scripture, and you can decide on ways in which the guests in the congregation can be involved too, either by joining in the choir or doing readings.

If a commissioned eucharistic minister is present, he/she can assist in the distribution of Holy Communion.

Wedding Booklets or Marriage Leaflets

There is an official Nuptial Mass and Rite of Marriage Leaflet supplied by the church. The hymns are, "Come O Creator Spirit Blessed," "Receive O Father in Thy Love" and "Christ be Beside Me."

Many couples have their own wedding booklets printed and personalised. These range from simple to state of the art.

You can have gold/silver lettering, the crest of the families, photographs/tassles, etc.

Customs

If you have a particular custom you'd like incorporated into your ceremony it can probably be arranged.

The wedding candle is a popular custom. Two candles are lit on the altar by the couple when they arrive to be married. After they exchange their vows, they take a candle each and together light the special wedding candle and blow out the separate candles.

Done in silence this is a tremendously stark symbol of the new status of the married couple, two but one. Wedding candles are available or you could make your own or buy an ordinary candle and decorate it with flowers and Christian symbols.

You keep the wedding candle and light it on special occasions, like your wedding anniversary or maybe in an hour of darkness to give hope.

At a wedding I attended the deceased parents of the groom were remembered with an inscription of their names on the chalice used for the wedding ceremony. The chalice was donated to an African mission church after the wedding. It was a moving, understated way to include the absent couple.

The Interdenominational Marriage

The term mixed marriage is now considered politically incorrect, interdenominational being the preferred word. When a Catholic wishes to marry a baptised person of another church, they must get permission from the Chancellery in the Archbishop's House in Dublin or the Diocesan bishop outside Dublin.

When a Catholic wishes to marry a non-baptised person they must get a dispensation from the Archbishop or Diocesan bishop.

Prior to the granting of permission or dispensation, the couple must undertake a series of instruction talks with the Catholic priest, after which permission or the dispensation is obtained when the Catholic partner writes to the bishop and the Archbishop writes back to the priest. Although the dispensation is no longer dependent on the promise of the children being brought up as Catholic, question eight on the Pre-nuptial Enquiry Form does ask: "Do you promise to do what you can, within the unity of your partnership, to

Marry with Taste

have all the children of your marriage baptised and brought up in the Catholic faith?"

A senior administrator in the Catholic Church tells me that Catholics are only asked to rear their children as Catholics within the unity of the partnership. What that means is, if the non-Catholic party was to say that they would break up the marriage if the child was to be christened a Catholic, then it's OK for the child to be reared non-Catholic.

Any couple experiencing difficulty in relation to missing documentation needed for their marriage should apply to the priest in the parish for help or failing that, the Chancellery in the Archbishop's House in Dublin or the local Diocesan bishop outside of Dublin.

The following is an extract from *Preparing for a Mixed Marriage*, published by Veritas for the Irish Episcopal Conference, 1983:

"As a general principle the Church discourages mixed marriages because they involve certain difficulties and tensions. This does not mean, however, that the Church will in any way seek to place obstacles in your path.

"You are not a 'general principle' but a couple who at this stage share a great deal at the level of affection and mutual understanding."

The general rule is that the Catholic must marry in a Catholic church, or to use the technical term, according to the canonical form. Whether you have a Mass or not is a matter of choice.

The non-Catholic party may decide against a Mass on the grounds that their family members might feel excluded from parts of the ceremony.

On the other hand, if the non-Catholic family were to interpret the omission of Nuptial Mass as expressing any lack of fraternal feeling towards them as fellow Christians, then obviously Mass should be celebrated. The couple, with their families, must decide.

Papal Blessing

If you want to have your Papal Blessing in time for your wedding you will need to allow at least three months.

The Papal Blessing is a decorative chart signed in Rome, by the Pope, a symbol of his blessing and of the prayerful support of the whole church.

Ask the priest in your parish for a letter of recommendation, which you bring to a Veritas shop where you choose from a selection of patterns. Veritas then send the chart to Rome.

Registering the Marriage

Find out beforehand from the minister who will assist you at the wedding, or from a priest in the parish where the wedding will take place, whose responsibility it is to register the marriage with the civil authority.

In the Republic of Ireland, if you are under twenty-one years of age civil law requires that you have the written consent of your parents.

Choosing the Day

Customs differ county to county. In Dublin, Sunday weddings are forbidden because of the pressure of priests just to attend their Sabbath duties.

I've been informed by a Catholic Church administrator that evening weddings are not allowed because:
(a) they could clash with funerals
(b) the church wants to discourage people from simply taking a few hours off work to get married.

In Meath and Kildare and many quiet parishes around the country, it is possible to get married on Sunday.

Marry with Taste

Weddings are forbidden on holy days in Dublin for the same reason as they are forbidden on Sunday. Nationwide, weddings are forbidden on some holy days, in Lent and Advent.

The Pre-marriage Programme

The pre-marriage programme is compulsory in most counties, except Dublin. The reason it's not compulsory in Dublin has nothing to do with religion, rather is it a logistical one, there are not enough places on pre-marriage courses to cater for the demand.

If for any reason the couple are unable or unwilling to attend a pre-marriage course then a number of "fireside" meetings can be arranged with a suitable married couple from a similar background to your own, or with the priest who will perform the marriage ceremony.

An engaged encounter is a weekend away with other engaged couples for informal talks and religious preparation.

For reservations contact: Mrs Kathleen O'Toole, Course Director, DOMAS, 16 North Great Georges Street, Dublin 1, Ph 786156/331300.

Checklist for the Marriage in the Catholic Church

- Is documentation complete:

- Has the marriage course been booked:

- Have wedding booklets been ordered:

- Printer:

- To be delivered:

- Price agreed:

- How many:

- Do we want a special custom:

- Has candle/chalice/been ordered:

- Have readings been sent to readers:

- What is the order for the musical arrangements:

- Has the time/date been set for the sacrament of reconciliation:

- Who will take the rings to church:

- Who will give out Mass booklets:

- Who will deliver offerings to the priest, sacristan, servers, soloist, choir, organist:

MARRYING IN GALWAY CATHEDRAL

If you'd like a bit of pomp and ceremony, why not get married in the cathedral nearest to your home? It's not an option for Dubliners whose Pro-Cathedral is open only to its parishioners, although they are allowed to marry in the small oratory. Galway Cathedral, resplendent in it's newness, is a different kettle of fish. Couples are made to feel welcome with an explanatory note which explains the necessary procedure to be followed, the first leg of which is to send for, fill out and return to the Cathedral, the special marriage particulars form.

The particulars required are the usual names and addresses, occupations, total number of bridal party, officiating priest.

The couple must then, through their own parish priest, arrange for the usual nuptial documentation, get written permission from the bride's parish priest for the marriage to take place in the Cathedral, if the Cathedral is not her parish, plus a certificate of attendance at a pre-marriage course.

MARRYING IN THE PRO-CATHEDRAL

Twenty thousand people pass through Dublin's Pro Cathedral every week. Probably because of such large numbers, only parishioners are allowed to marry in Saint Mary's Pro-Cathedral. Non-parishioners may, however, marry in St Kevin's, the small side oratory at Thomas' Lane, Dublin which seats about one hundred people.

Whether you want to marry in St Mary's or St Kevin's, you must apply in writing, giving names, addresses, home parishes and the name of the priest arranging the marriage papers, to the Administrator of the Pro-Cathedral, not later than three months before the proposed date of the wedding. Later than that and you'll need an explanatory letter from your local priest.

If you live outside the Pro-Cathedral parish you must supply your own priest for the wedding.

Send the completed documents to the Administrator at least two weeks before the date of the wedding.

Flowers: Delivered to the sacristy the afternoon before the wedding.

Music: Either engage the organist/musician of your choice or the Cathedral organist, for a fee of £25.

Ensure the music is from the approved repertoire of music. To avoid mistakes and disappointment, scour through the official list of non-liturgical music that is listed in the chapter on Music.

Give advance notice of your musical selection to the organist.

The good news for parishioners of the Pro-Cathedral is that there is no charge for them at St Kevin's. For non-parishioners the fee is £30, with an additional minimum £10 fee, for the Pro-Cathedral sacristan.

Marry with Taste

Before the ceremony, the best man must give the sacristan two envelopes, one marked, "Pro-Cathedral," the other, "Sacristan."

Wedding parties are asked specifically not to throw confetti in or near the chapel.

THE CHURCH OF IRELAND

❦

If both parties are member of the Church of Ireland, the banns may be read out in both parish churches three times. If there is no objection, the wedding goes ahead without further ado.

Instead of the reading of banns, a licence may be obtained from the diocesan registrar or a clergyman appointed by the bishop to issue licences and known as a "surrogate."

The Church of Ireland priest conducting the wedding service acts in place of the civil registrar; the service is both religious and civil.

If both people are baptised but only one person is a member of the Church of Ireland, a licence must be obtained from the diocesan registrar, or by his surrogate. The couple go to the registrar and the diocesan registrar and the Church of Ireland member swears on behalf of both that they are eligible to get married. If neither party has a claim or residency to get the licence, the service has to be in the Church in which you are resident or attend.

If that does not apply, go to the diocesan registrar and apply for a special licence which can only be given by the bishop of the diocese. You are required to swear an oath before a peace commissioner, in order to get permission to marry in a place or church. All marriages with the Church of Ireland have to be conducted by a priest.

A member of the Church of Ireland wishing to marry a non-baptised person will be referred to the registry office and the married couple are offered a blessing in the Church of Ireland.

There is a special licence which can be obtained for

special circumstances, if, for instance, a person needs to marry outside a church, say in their own home.

Second Marriages

The Church of Ireland doesn't forbid divorce. It is against the expressed wishes of the House of Bishops, but not the actual laws of the Church of Ireland, providing both parties are eligible to be married by the laws of the state. Clergy should not be placed in an embarrassing position by being requested to carry out such a ceremony. The couple are encouraged to remarry in the registry office again, after which the married couple can be blessed in the church.

Dr Rev Norman Gamble from Malahide Church of Ireland took time off to tell me exactly how he conducts a wedding service stressing that others in his congregation may do things differently:
"We encourage a couple to do a pre-marriage course, if possible, but we don't oblige them because many of our couples live long distances apart and it is not practicable. I usually see the couple on a number of occasions when readings are chosen, but don't issue a licence until three months beforehand. Hymns are sung by the congregation, secular songs or music is not allowed and would seldom, if ever, be requested. This is foremost a church ceremony. I allow no Flash Harry photographers during the service. I've attended wedding ceremonies where the intrusion of the photographer completely detracted from the solemnity of the occasion. If arranged in advance, I do allow photographs to be taken at the non-liturgical parts of the ceremony, such as when the bride is coming up the aisle or signing the register. But after the ceremony any desired shots can be re-enacted, putting on the ring, whatever."

MARRYING IN A METHODIST CHURCH

❦

As well as getting married in the registry office, members of the Methodist Church may be wed under one of three authorities:

1. By Special Licence which may be obtained on application to the Secretary of the Conference, Rev Edmund TJ Mawhinney, 1 Fountainville Ave, Belfast BT9 6AN, Ph (0232) 324554, Fax (0232) 239467.

2. By Ordinary Licence which may be obtained by serving notice on the Registrar of the District concerned.

3. By Registrar's Certificate, without Licence, which also may be obtained by serving notice on the Registrar of the District concerned.

The Marriage by Certificate must be solemnised under similar conditions to those required for marriage by Ordinary Licence.

Before a marriage can be solemnised in any Methodist Church, the church must be duly registered for that purpose by the Registrar-General of Northern Ireland or of the Republic of Ireland. Registration is obtained by the following procedure:

The officiating minister, trustee or owner of the church, must certify, in writing, to the Registrar-General that the building is used as a place of public worship by a congregation of the Methodist Church.

The minister, trustee or owner certifying, must give the Registrar-General a certificate signed by ten householders that this church has been used by them, during one year, at least, as their usual place of public worship, and that they are desirous that it be registered for solemnising marriages. The minister, trustee or owner then counter-signs the certificate.

On the receipt of the certificate, the Registrar-General shall register the church in the General Registry Office and shall send a certificate of registration to the person certifying and to the Registrar of the District in which the church is situated.

The fee for registration must be paid at the time of delivery of the certificates to the Registrar-General.

Every application for the substitution and registry of a new church or building, in place of a disused one, shall be made to the Registrar-General through the Registrar of the District. The fee for the substitution is payable to the Registrar of the District.

Marriage where one of the Parties Resides out of Ireland

There are specific regulations governing marriage ceremonies where one of the parties resides outside Ireland. Full particulars may be obtained from any District Registrar.

Means of Preventing Improper Marriages

The Registrar is required to send a copy of the Notice of the Marriage to the ministers of the places of worship which each party usually attends and of the place of worship in which the marriage is to be solemnised.

The onus is then on the ministers at the places of worship, which each party usually attends, to assure themselves that the contemplated marriage is not an improper one, and that parents and guardians are cognisant of it.

Any persons whose consent to the marriage of a minor if necessary may, without fee, forbid the issue of the Registrar's Certificate by writing in the Marriage Notice Book, the word "forbidden," and signing his or her name and address, and the character in respect of which he or she is so authorised. The persons authorised to give consent to minors are listed in the regulations governing the solemnisation of marriages. Anyone can enter a caveat against the issue of the Registrar's Licence or Certificate. The caveat must be signed by or on behalf of the person who enters it and must state the ground of objection on which it is founded. Caution is advised, any person entering a caveat on frivolous grounds is liable to an action.

MARRYING IN THE REGISTRY OFFICE

❦

The Dublin Registry Office is at 31 Molesworth Street, Dublin 2.

In recent years the number of couples choosing the registry office rather than a church for their marriage has increased to an average of one couple a day.

Their choice may be due to a lack of religious commitment or because either party is divorced and therefore cannot be remarried in a Catholic church.

In order to marry in a registry office you must reside within the District of the Registry Office for fourteen days. On the fifteenth day Notice of Marriage can be served on the Registrar and the ceremony can take place on the eighth day after that.

If the marriage is to take place on the Authority of the Registrar's Certificate, it's necessary that each party should have resided within the district of the Registrar to whom the Notice is given for the space of seven days immediately preceding the giving of the Notice of the Marriage. On the twenty-second day from the date of entering of the Notice, a certificate may be issued by the Registrar and the ceremony can take place on or after that date.

If neither party has been attending a place of worship for one month prior to the Notice of Marriage being given, i.e. if the banns have not been read out in a church, a special Notice must be inserted in a newspaper. The wording of the Notice will be supplied by the registry office. Complete copies of the newspapers containing the said notice must be produced prior to the wedding taking place.

If either party has been married previously it will be necessary for that party to produce either a Death

Certificate or a divorce Decree Absolute and Birth Certificates of both parties to the divorce, if born outside the state.

Two questionnaires in relation to both parties to the divorce must be completed - these will be given at the time of the serving of the Notice. The registrar will forward this statement to the Registrar General whose permission must be obtained before the ceremony can take place. This normally takes five to six weeks.

If either party is under the age of twenty-one, the written consent of both parents of the party concerned must be obtained. A Form of Consent will be given to the parties which must be signed and witnessed and returned before the ceremony takes place.

If either party is under the age of sixteen years an application for permission to marry must be made to the president of the High Court.

The registrar's fee is never more than £32.50 which includes the outlay and a copy of the Marriage Certificate after the ceremony has taken place. When Notices in a newspaper are required the amount payable to the newspapers will also be due.

The wedding ceremony can take place not less than eight days and not more than three months after the Notice of Marriage has been given. An appointment is necessary to serve Notice of Marriage.

The marriage can take place any day, Monday to Friday, between the hours of 9.30 a.m. and 12.30 p.m. and 2.30 p.m. and 4.30 p.m.

The Accessories

Flowers

The Registry Office has its own floral arrangement but that needn't stop you from bringing in your own arrangements if desired.

Marry with Taste

Capacity

Twenty-five to thirty guests can be comfortably accommodated, more mean squeeze.

Music

While there is no musical instrument available at the Registry Office, most couples bring their own ranging from sophisticated hi-tech equipment to the simple tape deck.

Red Carpet

As in a church the red carpet is rolled the day of the marriage and collected immediately afterwards.

Witnesses

You can bring the witnesses of your choice, gather in two passers-by over sixteen years of age, or the staff in the Registry Office, being seasoned witnesses are always willing to oblige.

Any enquires to Olive Dawson, Ph 6763218.

MARRYING OUTSIDE THE PARISH

Why People Choose this Option

1. <u>For Snob Reasons</u>

Though not by any means a stampede, there is an increase in the number of couples who marry outside their local church for a variety of reasons, ranging from the frivolous to the religious to the frankly snobbish. I can remember the hurt and bewilderment of some of my relatives when their most famous nephew, of whom they were so proud, decided against marrying in his local parish and chose instead the chapel in Trinity College despite the fact that neither he nor his bride were graduates of TCD. The fact that he had shunned the local church was viewed as an act of rejection motivated by pure snobbery.

2. <u>For Architectural Design</u>

Another couple I know scoured Wicklow until they found an architecturally pleasing small granite church, in just the right scenic location, to provide a spectacular backdrop for the video.

If you are going to marry outside your parish church it's best to have either a local friendly clergyman or a very good reason, preferably with a religious connotation, as to why you are deserting your own parish.

Most priests like weddings; they're happy, cheerful occasions they are also a small source of revenue, so don't be surprised if the local priest expresses regret when you announce you're going to wed at St Elsewhere.

3. For a Human-friendly Scale

Some parishes have huge cavernous churches which ring hollow with emptiness, even with a wedding party of two hundred. Small churches are in demand, like the one in Kinsealy, to afford an intimacy which is more conducive to the wedding ceremony.

4. The Setting

Churches, especially some in very busy city centre roads, have people ambling around them all day which can prove a distraction for those at the wedding.

5. The Continuum

When I got an invitation to the wedding of a friend's daughter, I assumed the marriage would take place in Malahide because both the bride and groom had been baptised, made their communion and confirmation, and were still living in Malahide.

The night before the wedding I checked the invitation, just to make sure it was at 2 p.m. Quite by chance, I noticed Church of the Precious Blood and knowing that wasn't the name of the Catholic Church in Malahide, I looked again to see Cabra, Dublin 7.

It turned out that soon after the couple met they discovered that both of their grandparents had been married in the Church of the Precious Blood in Cabra.

The marriage proposal was made when he suggested they should follow in their grandparents' footsteps and make the Cabra Connection. And so history was repeated.

Why Marry Abroad?

The reasons why people choose to marry in foreign countries as opposed to foreign parishes is different again. It could be to ensure the minimum of fuss, it could be a way of getting away from unwanted, albeit caring, if clawing relatives. While it's seldom a way of saving money, it is a way of ensuring that you spend your money on what you really want instead of spending it by following a tradition, for no better reason, than because it is a tradition.

Some couples marry in Rome and Fatima for religious reasons. From my own straw pole, such couples are very much in the minority.

How to Marry in Rome

It's easy to understand why the Eternal City of Rome is such a popular choice for foreign weddings for the people of Ireland. It's near. In Ireland you are always only a stone's throw or a telephone call away from someone who knows someone who knows a priest in Rome. Failing that, your parish priest or travel agent will have a contact. As well as being the universal nerve centre of Catholicism, it's at the centre of Europe. In fact, travel agents tell me that most of the couples who marry in Rome leave it a day or two later and honeymoon elsewhere.

For a Catholic wedding in Rome or anywhere else outside Ireland, there are certain extra arrangements to be made. The initial step in all cases is to make contact, either by phone or by letter, with a priest in the parish in which you wish to marry.

You then go to your own local priest with the name and address of the priest in the foreign parish. The local priest will arrange your pre-nuptial papers and send these on to the priest abroad.

If you wish to marry in Rome write to the Irish College:

The Rector, Pontificio Collegio Irlandese,
Via Santi Quattro 1, 00184 Roma, Italy.

Ph 7315697, prefix 16396, when phoning from Ireland.

Marry with Taste

How to Marry in France

Because of a residency clause which requires the couple to spend eight days in France before the wedding, many couples perform the civil ceremony in Ireland before going to France for the religious ceremony. When you write or phone the Irish College, you will get a letter and a special form to fill in. As well as arranging the religious end of things you must also tie the knot, legally speaking.

At least three months, preferably sooner, before the wedding, contact the Department of Foreign Affairs, who will send a form to be completed. The Department will, through the relevant Embassy, issue a document to the designated priest in Rome.

When the church documents are completed for both the bride and groom, they are sent, by your local priest, to the diocesan offices to be verified. The documents are then forwarded to the priest in Rome who will perform the marriage.

The priest in Rome must wait until he has all these documents before he can set in motion the arrangements needed for the wedding.

There are hundreds of churches in Rome. Most weddings take place near to the Irish College because that's where the couple go to sign the register. In 1993, when I visited the Basilica in Rome, I chanced upon a couple in full nuptial regalia, with a trail of wedding guests. I found out that among Romans it is a custom to visit the Basilica on their wedding day to pay homage and to take photgraphs.

Remember, the marriage certificate must be translated into English if you want to use it to procure a mortgage.

The Cost: About £1,000 for flight and accommodation, £150 for the priest and the Irish College.

TREASA BROGAN

How to get Hitched in Haiti

You know that foreign weddings have really become commonplace when you see them advertised in the Golden Pages.

Frank Constantine of Sandymount Travel Ltd, 4 Seafort Avenue, Dublin 4, Ph 6684399, tells me that for £3,500 a couple can marry and stay for two weeks in exotic locations like Grenada, Barbados, Mauritius, Antigua, Orlando, Kenya, Far East and the Caribbean.

"We arrange the wedding, witnesses, the hotel, the cake, the lot. We have contacts with the Catholic Church in all of these countries for the couple wishing to marry in a Catholic Church. We also arrange non-Catholic weddings, in fact, fifty per cent of our clients are non-Catholic. It takes about three and a half months from the inquiry to take off.

"It's not our brief to advise people how to run their lives but we prefer if a couple have fully thought through the implications of the foreign wedding, as we often find that spur of the minute inquiries which seem very romantic at the time, often have to be abandoned or reconsidered because of personal circumstances.

"Foreign weddings are not always small quiet affairs. One of our couples who married in a hotel in Mauritius, were surprised and delighted to discover that the owner of the hotel had laid on champagne and cake for everyone staying in the hotel, and what had been planned as a small wedding turned into a huge shindig."

"Are foreign weddings legally binding in Ireland?" I asked Frank.

"The best answer I can give you is that we have been informed by the Department of Foreign Affairs that a wedding which takes place under the normal rules and regulations of a foreign country, is legally binding here."

The Civil Marriage Certificate

As it is the civil marriage certificate that is required for a mortgage, and not the church certificate, it will be necessary to have the civil marriage certificate translated into English if the couple wish to buy a house in Ireland.

WHO PAYS FOR WHAT?

I know a well-paid, miserly executive who never as much as bought a dental filling for his only son. Not surprisingly, when the young man married, the father didn't break the habit of a lifetime and suddenly become flaithiúlach with his money and buy a round of drinks, or anything.

The moral of the story is, there are traditions, and there are families and there's money and who pays for what depends very much on how the family functions and who can afford to pay for what.

The onset of equality and the soaring costs of weddings has more or less put an end to the tradition that the bride's family must foot the bill.

It's reckoned that at least half, if not more couples, pay or greatly contribute to the financing of their own wedding. However, many still do it the the traditional way.

The Groom

Pays for all of the flowers
Engagement/Engagement announcements/
Wedding ring
His own wedding clothes or the hire of formal clothes for himself/best man
Legal costs
Presents for the best man
Certificates/licences
The stag
Transport
The honeymoon

Marry with Taste

The Bride

Bridesmaid's outfits and presents
Ring for groom and present
Hen party

The Bride's Father

Wedding dress
Reception
Stationery
Photography
Video

Groom's Parents

May offer to supply drink for wedding day or for breakfast and toast

The Best Man

Own suit, if not in formal wear

DUTIFUL ATTENDANTS

Duties of the Best Man

Best men are usually chosen because they are the brother or the best friend of the groom. But weddings run smoothest when they are executed with full military precision. On the wedding day, the best man is the pivotal person who sees to it that details dovetail in this operatic-scale, orchestration of departures and arrivals, as planned. The best man's success or failure in executing these duties will produce either melodious music or mayhem. Ergo, don't mind whether he's as handsome as Gabriel Byrne or as rich as Michael Smurfit, what you really need is a best man who combines the charm and cunning of PJ Mara at a Fianna Fáil Ard Fhéis.

The Best Man's Duties are to:

Organise the stag night and ensure the groom survives it.
Help the groom choose the wedding clothes.
Make sure the wedding clothes are collected and/or laid out.
Bring the bride and groom's overnight case and going away clothes to the bridal suite at the reception venue.
Organise and attend the church rehearsal.
The most important duty—ensure the groom gets to the church on time, or preferably fifteen minutes early.
Soothe the groom's nerves while he awaits his bride.
Delegate duties among the ushers at the church.

Marry with Taste

Bring the buttonholes to the church if required.
Take care of the rings and hand them over during the ceremony.
Pay the church fees, the priest, altar boys, choir, soloist.
Walk with the chief bridesmaid out of the church, behind the bride and groom and attendants.
Ensure that everyone at the wedding has transport to the reception.
Take care of his own transport to the reception.
Is part of the receiving line.
Give a chucklingly charming speech ending with a toast for the bridesmaids.
Take charge of the groom's clothes after the wedding, returning them, if necessary, to the hire company.
Announce the departure of the bride and groom and maybe produce the groom's "hidden" car at the last moment.

The Duties of the Bridesmaid

The chief bridesmaid, she who witnesses the register, was traditionally the bride's sister. Now best friends are often first choice or the groom's sister. If a sister is not being chosen she should be told after the chosen bridesmaid has agreed, and before anyone else knows of the arrangements. Weddings can turn into notorious emotional battle grounds; eliminating trouble before it begins gets things off to a good start.

If the chief bridesmaid is married, then she is given the clinical term of Matron of Honour.

While the bridesmaid's duties are not anything as onerous as those of the best man, and are often executed by other members of the family, it's best to choose someone with a generous helpful nature rather than a look-at-me ego-tripper.

The Bridesmaid's Duties are to:

Help the bride choose her trousseau.
Arrange the "hen party", including any surprise happenings, at least one week prior to the wedding.
Help choose dresses for herself and young attendants.
Stay overnight at the bride's home to help dress the bride.
Keep the bride calm.
Help the bride with make up and hair, if necessary.
Join the receiving line.
Check that the bride's going away outfit and overnight bag has been put into the charge of the best man.
Go to the church before the bride, check the attendants are poised to perfection, with head-dresses in place and bouquets just so.
Give the last minute OK to the bride before she walks up the aisle.
Take the bouquet during the ceremony and lift back the blusher veil after the "I do's," have been said.
Witness the signing of the register.
Leave the church on the arm of the best man, behind the young attendants.
Take care of the young bridesmaids at reception.
Help the bride to change into the going away outfit.
Ensure the wedding dress is safely delivered to the bride's mother.

The Receiving Line

In recent years the formal receiving line has been replaced by informal instructions. Despite the formality of it, a receiving line does ensure that everyone meets the bride and groom at least once. I never met the groom at the last wedding I attended and wouldn't know him if I passed him on the street. Seems strange.

Marry with Taste

Arrange for both sets of parents, with the bride and groom and maybe chief bridesmaid and best man (the more people on the receiving line the quicker it will pass, as people move to the people they know), to take up positions inside the door as the guests file into the formal reception, after the sherry reception. The guests will be so hungry, they'll want to find their place at the table, they won't want to hang around talking, so you'll find their determination to be fed will set a brief but nonetheless polite agenda for the introductions.

It's at this stage that you could ask everyone to sign a register, an invaluable record in later years.

The Wedding Breakfast

Whether you have a marquee or hotel reception, the usual layout is either an E-shape with the bridal party at the top table in full view of all the guests, or a straight table surrounded by small round tables or a half moon cluster of round tables with one top table.

The Top Table:

Grandparents
Best man
Groom's mother
Bride's father
Bride
Groom
Bride's mother
Groom's father
Priest
Grandparents

THE HONEYMOON

"My love, we will go, we will go, I and you,
And away in the woods we will scatter the dew:
And the salmon behold, and the ousel too,
My love, I and you, we will hear, we will hear,
The calling afar of the doe and the deer,
And the bird in the branches will cry for us clear,
And the cuckoo unseen in his festival mood:
And death, oh my fair one, will never come near,
In the bosom afar of the fragrant wood."
   Love song from the Gaelic
   translated by WB Yeats

The honeymoon is another part of the marriage ritual which has gone back to the future in terms of destination. For many couples the dew scattered is more than likely to be local dew and not at all "in the bosom afar of the fragrant woods."

Whether the reasons are social, economic or due to changing lifestyles, the honeymoon is no longer the big set piece at the end of the wedding day, as it used to be.

With the exception of two, all of the couples I talked to when compiling this book had opted for a weekend or a one night honeymoon with the intention of doing something special later on, presumably when the wedding day expenses had been overcome.

But most couples need some sort of a holiday after their marriage, the physical and emotional strain of the lead up to the wedding day takes a toll. If it is at all possible, honeymoon and be damned.

Whether you go to the utterly idyllic Isle of Bali, off the Indonesian coast (fly Garuda out of London for about £1,000 each), or, like me, experience the magical celtic mists of the Isle of Inisheer (the smallest of the Aran Islands), the honeymoon plan must be in place at least weeks prior to the wedding day.

If you plan to marry in the high season make sure to book well in advance. Choose a travel agent who is a member of the Travel Agents Association, and therefore insured against unforeseen events and take out insurance against your own holiday being cancelled.

This ensures that you are covered both ways. If the holiday company goes you won't lose out; if you have to cancel, you will only lose a small amount, as against all of your honeymoon money.

If you are going away to exotic lands, you'll need to have arranged injections, immunisation. Few couples go away on the wedding night. Most stay either in the hotel where the reception is being held, or in a nearby hotel. Indeed most hotels include a complementary overnight stay for the bride and groom, which I am reliably informed is mainly availed of on the wedding night; champagne, flowers, and the bridal suite are often included.

I know a hotel, to remain nameless, which lays on a service around midnight of driving the couple off in the hotel's bridal car. Once there is no one following, the car simply drives around to the tradesman's entrance and the couple are led to the bridal suite with all the collusion of a "colleen bawn" scenario.

Going on honeymoon the day after the wedding gives the couple a chance to recover from the festivities of the day before making a long haul across the globe. Whether you go on the day of, or on the day after, the wedding, the cases will have to be packed before the wedding, containing the documents, passports, travellers cheques or foreign currency.

Going on honeymoon alone or in company is optional. The last wedding I attended the couple went off on holiday to Latvia, with hundreds of others, to see Ireland's soccer team in action! If you are the type who would love an exotic honeymoon but cannot afford a wedding and a honeymoon, why not reverse the trend and have a honeymoon wedding.

The honeymoon wedding involves a lot of travel for the couple, with or without guests.

In some cases the couple and suitably selected and agreeable guests (agreeable in that they are available to travel) all pack their back packs and head for a week in Provence, the Galway Races, a cruise on the Shannon, or block book an independent hostel, the options are endless. The marriage can take place quietly before the trekking begins.

In another version of the honeymoon wedding, the couple travel to say America to be married among friends and relatives, then, having packed the video and the top tier of the wedding cake they set off on a globe-trotting tour of more relatives and friends, where the video of the wedding is viewed until the honeymooners run out of cousins, comrades, continents or cake.

Honeymoon Checklist

- Has accommodation been arranged for wedding night:

- Where:

- Who will bring us:

- Where has car been left:

- Who has suitcases, passports, money:

- Who will take the going away cases to the reception venue:

- Honeymoon booked with:

- Contact:

- Time of flight:

- Are visas necessary:

- Do we need immunisation:

And So To Wed...

ADRIAN AND JACKIE SHINE

I don't know how it will sound in years to come when their children and grandchildren ask about their wedding day, and they have to answer, well, we thought about it for a long time, but it wasn't until we won a wedding that we finally took the plunge.

Marriage has always been regarded as an event that involves the community, but I don't think I've ever heard of anyone who took that premise quite so literally, as Adrian and Jackie Shine, whose marriage in July 1993 had all the pomp, pagentry and mayhem of a Mardi Gras carnival.

They had been engaged for four years. Adrian admitted, "I was a bit scared of marriage and then we never seemed to have the money."

Jackie, from Birr, Co Offaly, has a sister living in Kells, and herself and Adrian often spent weekends there. It was on such a visit that they saw the "Win-a-Wedding" sign.

Jackie: "The Kells 800 Committee were organising a festival to celebrate the eight hundred year old Church Priory. At first, the committee intended to hold a mock medieval wedding as the culmination of the festival week, but then someone decided that a real medieval wedding would be better, so the search went out for a couple who would be prepared to marry on a certain date, dressed in medieval clothes, eating medieval food, with medieval music, the whole shebang. We talked about it for a while, then we forgot about it."

Adrian butts in: "I don't think we forgot it. I remember saying to you that you didn't seem very interested in the competition and you said you didn't think I was interested in getting married. There and then we decided that win or lose the wedding competition, we would get married."

As it happened, a lot of couples showed initial interest, but when push came to shove, only six couples were really prepared to participate in a marriage more like a community pageant than a private celebration.

Adrian admits they are both competitive, in fact, he used to subscribe to an English competition winning magazine. They decided that if they were going to go for it, they would put in a lot of effort.

Three couples were picked to go on stage in front of an audience, in a sort of Rose of Tralee interview.

"We were interviewed by the local tourist guy and four people from the village. I had my joke ready and that proved a good start. They asked us if we'd comply with all the arrangements the festival intended to make on our behalf and if we'd take our glasses off for the day. We agreed. Jackie sang "Summertime" and I accompanied her on an imaginary trumpet, we got a big cheer from all of the friends we had planted in the audience and we won."

The prize included a meal and the hire of medieval clothes for thirty guests, a parade with float, musicians, and a honeymoon of seven nights, in seven castles in Ireland and more.

They were to be married twelve weeks later, on 17th July 1993.

"That's less than the mandatory three months," Adrian told me. "My priest in Dublin said, 'Listen, if you have any trouble with the priest in Kells, let me know. I'll sort it out.' Then the priest in Kells said, 'Listen, if you have any trouble with the priest in Dublin, let me know, I'll sort it out.' Between Kells, Dublin and Birr we were well sorted.

"With so much to do, the twelve weeks seemed like twelve months. On the wedding morning I played golf

Marry with Taste

with the best man and groomsmen. I figured it was the best way to keep them out of the pub. It worked.

"It was also the first time in weeks I could forget the wedding for one hour. We had asked all of our friends and relatives to dress suitably. A lot of them did and it really added so much to our day. In fact, the ones who didn't said later they regretted not joining in. You can do anything when you are dressed up. It's a sort of mask.

"There was one awkward moment when some of the guests, dressed in civvies shall we say, sat in the front row of the church. The church in Kells holds one hundred and fifty people. It's small. So for the video, we wanted medieval dress only in the front two rows. The jester, doubling up as the usher, dressed in black and red, with a black and red face and a powder puff baton, bonked these guests on the head with the baton and sent them down to the back row for being dressed improperly. Everyone laughed.

"We got all of the clothes in the Dublin Costume Company and they were really exceptionally beautiful. It cost £500 for twenty outfits. I wore white knee length socks, a green Henry VIII velvet dress, green velvet jacket with gold braid. The best man and groomsmen were dressed as Nottingham sheriffs and courtiers. We were married by the parish priest of Kells, Monsignor Campion. He was very good. He managed to get very old vestments which were buff coloured and they might as well have been medieval."

Tempting fate to a daring degree, Jackie chose an Anne Boleyn dress. One can only hope it won't prove prophetic.

Jackie says: "It was absolutely beautiful, creamy coloured, waisted with a huge puff sleeve and gold braiding. The headpiece was a delicate filigree tiara. The bridesmaid's were in deep rich colours; green and black and mauves. No, it didn't look sombre. In fact, the colours just danced out at you. All the gold braiding had a stunning sumptuous effect.

"My father is the propagator in Birr Castle. He made me a sheaf of blue flowers; very traditional, unfussy. Although they were taped at the bottom, they looked as if they had just been freshly cut."

Adrian's nervousness took him by surprise. "We got married at three and I've never been so nervous in my life. Normally I talk the hind legs off a donkey, but I stuttered and muttered and the sweat rolled off me. Luckily by the time it came to making a speech I had recovered.

"During the ceremony, the festival choir sang Latin hymns and Gregorian chants. After the church ceremony a prancing/dancing jester let the parade through the town of Kells, headed by forty locals, in medieval dress, on horseback, followed by a troupe of medieval musicians from Galway playing lutes and lyres. We came next in a horse-drawn carriage, and a float behind us carried the bridesmaids, groomsmen and anyone dressed appropriately who had managed to jump on.

"The reception was in a marquee overlooking the eight hundred year old Priory. That's where we took the photographs. As well as the invited guests, the festival committee had sold tickets at £25 a head to anyone who wished to join in the celebration, once they were suitably attired. So we ended up with about 400 at the reception.

"The medieval banquet began with a pig on the spit, King's River salmon, followed by haunch of heifer and strawberries and cream. The Mount Juliet band played and minuets were executed to varying degrees of daintiness."

Adrian and Jackie agree that while absolutely everything about the marquee reception was great, toilet facilities were a definite drawback.

Marry with Taste

"We skipped the first night of our honeymoon because we didn't want to miss the craic. We stayed instead at a secret bed and breakfast in Kells—we didn't want anyone putting straw or nettles in our bed. With one of the festival organisers, we were the last to leave the reception at 6 a.m. I don't think we'll ever forget it. You could say it was medieval magic."

Damien O'Leary and Heather O'Hare

The wedding of Damien O'Leary and Heather O'Hare was indeed a family and friends affair. Wheelchair-bound Heather absolutely hates shopping so she simply roped in her family and friends to do this tiresome chore, freeing her to concentrate on track training and therefore maintain her world placing. She is fourth in the world in the wheelchair 400 meters track event and fifth in the world in the 800 meters.

She got these placements in Barcelona in 1992 and with her sights set on Berlin in 1994, she didn't see why a mere marriage should interfere with the work that is needed to be done. Being involved with the timing for wheelchair track events, Damien nods in agreement.

Damien and Heather giggle a lot, conspiratorially, when they remember just how many people were roped in to help them organise their big day. Damien tells me, "Well, if we didn't do a lot of shopping for it, we certainly planned our day fairly meticulously and probably for that reason it went off very well and we both enjoyed it."

It was Damien who decided that they should hold their reception at ALSAA, the Aer Lingus Sports Association's function rooms, near Dublin Airport.

"I had used it for my twenty-first and knew that it was easily accessible for the wheelchair, it's a lovely venue and the food is great. You have to pick from a list of four specified caterers. My father is a member of ALSAA so he got the booking for me."

They met in college four and a half years ago where Heather was studying computers and Damien architectural drafting. Two years ago they booked Heather's local church, the Church of the Holy Child in

Marry with Taste

Whitehall, which again is wheelchair friendly.

"My sister got married two years ago. I liked her dress so much I decided it would be mine too. I friend very kindly offered to do the alterations to my own specifications. For instance, I wanted a straight line because I knew if there was too much material or bulk, it could get caught in the wheel as I was going up the aisle. I wanted it plain at the back too, you don't see the back of a dress in the wheelchair and the ornamentation would have been very uncomfortable. I bought lovely ballet shoes for £10, they set off the dress nicely."

Damien also got two new tyres for Heather's wheelchair.

"Another friend that I work with," she giggles again, "offered to make silk flowers for my head-dress and I had a short shoulder length veil which my sister got for me."

Heather showed me the top tier of the wedding cake. Like that of Sarah Ferguson and Prince Andrew, the initials were romantically linked at the corners. Heather told me her father made it. "He is a professional confectioner, he iced it too, it was really beautiful."

Damien's father has been making cine-films for years, so he offered to do the video. "The only thing he forgot were the speeches." They giggle again as Damien remembers the slagging his father got. "He was sitting at the top table, feeling so nervous, thinking about the speech he would have to make, he forgot to ask someone else to take over from him. We don't mind but we gave him a hard time."

Heather used the florist and the musicians engaged by her sister, two years ago, for her wedding. "Because we were planning our wedding then, we were watching out for the things for ourselves. The flowers cost £200 which included my bouquet, the two bridesmaids, the table settings and the buttonholes. I liked my own bouquet so much I wouldn't throw it. I threw the bridesmaid's instead. I had intended bringing my bouquet to my mother's grave but never got around to it. The band, Neat Beat, cost £275 and were very good. Two friends provided all of the music at the church. She sang and played the flute and he played the guitar. It was gentle and very moving. I particularly like the sound of the flute."

Damien organised the cars and the clothes for the men. "A friend of mine (he laughs), yes, we seem to know a lot of useful people, got me two Bentleys for £100. Now that's more than reasonable. I went to Black Tie for the men's clothes. It cost £165 for five suits. We had two fittings and everything was absolutely perfect.

"The ALSAA functions room costs £50 to hire, and the caterers start at £11. For £13 a head, we had two starters, turkey/ham, profiteroles, tea/coffee and a toast. We had 94 guests at the wedding breakfast and about 170 more people came to the evening do which cost only £1 per head, for finger sandwiches. ALSAA has all the comfort of a hotel function room and holds about 300 easily."

Neither being comfortable with the idea of a gift list and not wanting to tell people what to buy them, Damien may have hit on an even better idea. "Well, we didn't end up with four ironing boards anyway. When people asked us what we wanted, we said we didn't know. So we either got gift vouchers or cheques. We think that's a better idea than the gift list, because there's no storage problem, the bank looks after that end of things, and now that we have settled in we are enjoying getting everything gradually. No, it doesn't mean that Heather has started to shop, she just sees something somewhere and guess who goes and gets it?"

Heather and Damien honeymooned in Galway for a few days before heading off for yet another track event in Wales.

TOM AND FRANCES LAWLOR

Ace photographer, Tom Lawlor, met his wife, Frances, on a blind date. Since he got so many of the details wrong on the first telling, Frances decided to put the record straight.

"My sister Margaret arranged it. She was doing a line with a guy in the *Irish Times* where Tom worked. They were going out to celebrate her birthday. Tom had nothing to do and decided to join them, so I was asked along to make up the foursome. We went out together for two years; we always knew we'd get married some day. Then we bought the house in Clontarf. We were settling in nicely when one day, out of the blue, we were sitting here and we decided we wanted to get married.

"Tom contacted a priest he knew well and asked him what was the shortest period of time it would take to legally arrange a wedding. The priest said three weeks, and Tom asked him to arrange it.

"First there was my mother. She was horrified, couldn't understand the big hurry, especially, may I say, as I wasn't even pregnant. She told me I didn't know what I was doing. I told her that if I didn't know what I was doing at twenty-four, I'd never know. I seldom plan anything but I'm a logical thinker. I have a lot of common sense. If I have a good feeling about something I'll do it, if not I won't."

Tom remembers the objections of the priest in Portmarnock. "Let's say he wasn't exactly keen on the idea. He wanted us to wait until we did a pre-marriage course, but Tom told him absolutely no way. I told him we gave courses, we didn't take them. Eventually he acceded to our request and we got the necessary letter of freedom."

They both agree, that for them, it was the ideal way to get married. Frances told me, "It was great. No fuss, no long engagement, no waiting, dare I say it, no plan. The only thing we really had to have was the documentation, birth certificates, baptismal certificates, letters of freedom. I bought material, and had a tailor make up a two-piece cream suit. I picked the suit up from the tailor the night before the wedding. I bought a blouse in Arnotts, and I had the shoes. My younger sister was my bridesmaid. I bought her a long blue dress in the Bridal Department in Arnotts.

"On the way to University Church on the Green I picked up three orchids at the local florist, which Tom had ordered in advance. Tom's friend was best man. We got married at eleven o'clock on December 18th 1976. We had a wedding breakfast for thirty people, family and friends, at the King Sitric in Howth. No, we didn't have to plan that either, though we did have to book a table. Otherwise it was open menu, everyone chose what they wanted. We had no wedding cake.

"The photographer, Bill Doyle, a friend of Tom's, took the photographs. We spent a few hours in the King Sitric, after which we headed for our local pub, The Shed, where we had a couple of drinks.

"Some people went home. We went back to our house, went to bed for a few hours, got up, put on our jeans and sweaters and went back to The Shed and home again.

"That was Saturday, we stayed home alone on Sunday and Monday and then drove off in the car and ended up at the Talbot Hotel, Wexford, where we stayed for a few days before returning to Dublin for Christmas with Tom's family.

"It was great, I wouldn't have wanted it any other way." Tom and Frances have two daughters, Jenny, eleven and Deirdre, eight and a half.

Deirdre O'Kane and Stephen O'Connor

Deirdre O'Kane is the PRO of the Olympia Theatre. When she met Stephen O'Connor it was an apocalyptical, earth-shattering, love at first sight, scale.

"He came home with me that very night. He rang his mother next morning and when he told her what happened, her first reaction was, "But Stephen you have no clean shirt." He told his mother that a clean shirt was not exactly an urgent priority. She giggles as she remembers. Seven weeks later they decided to get married but it was not until six years, hundreds of shirts and one five-year-old daughter later, when they eventually fulfilled that early decision.

"Yes, you could say we are impulsive. In fact, we were buying our first house, mid-negotiations, with all the coming and goings which that undertaking involves, when we decided, one Thursday morning in 1988, that we really should put our commitment in a legal frame.

"We found out that the earliest possible day we could get married was eight days later on the following Friday week. We went down to the Registry Office to fill out forms and put the notices in the paper. We really didn't want a church wedding. Neither of us is religious, but we regarded getting married as a very serious commitment.

"We also regarded the whole business of a large reception as a terrific waste of money, especially when every penny we had was going into the new house. As well as that, I'd have to say, I've never been to a wedding I enjoyed. It always seems to me the bride and groom don't enjoy weddings either. By the time the bride has danced dutifully with every last arthritic uncle and grand-uncle, she's worn out. The music and whole general performance thing is geared to catering for the greatest number of people in varying age ranges.

"I believe young people prefer something different. We wanted a day we would enjoy. We contacted our immediate family, brothers, sisters, parents, and told them to be at the Registry Office at two o'clock Friday week.

"I rang most of the major hotels, and found their attitude to our small number appalling, they were simply not interested. But if we were a small party, we had plenty of money to lavish on a meal for fourteen.

"The Russell Court Hotel, in Harcourt Street, Ph 4784066, had a different attitude. As well as complementary overnight accommodation for the bride and groom, they offered a complementary horse and carriage service, which takes the newly-weds from the marriage venue to the Russell Court.

"I took the Thursday before my wedding day off work in order to shop for something suitable to wear. I got a gorgeous white suit for myself at a Richard Allen sale and a white and pink broderie anglaise dress for Sara, our five-year-old daughter who was to be ring-bearer. My mother supplied a huge wedding cake.

"On the Friday we drove ourselves to the Registry Office in our red Mini. We parked it off Molesworth Street. We were pleasantly surprised with the marriage service. We had thought it would be businesslike and brisk but the Registrar embued the ceremony with more meaning than I have ever heard before or since. In fact it turned out that the Registrar was conducting his last service (the incoming Registrar was present, observing all) and he really gave it his all.

"I can only describe our Registrar as a lost actor, such a deep, rich baritone voice would have earned him a fortune on stage.

"You know how some ministers use what is almost a

Marry with Taste

rhyming chant when they are conducting a wedding service. This was very different.

"I found the whole ceremony very emotional. Stephen's hands were shaking so much he nearly dropped the ring. We had both looked on this as a necessary procedure that we were going through, but we were both pleasantly surprised and delighted with the warmth of the service. I often think that mothers get overlooked at weddings, so we had our respective mothers as our witnesses, which added an unusual, if very appropriate touch.

"With the help of his tripod, Stephen took the photographs. They are very good. No video, I didn't want it. I think it best to remember the day as you want to remember it, the camera can have a cruel eye.

"My bouquet was a small very discreet affair, but then Stephen brought three dozen long-stemmed roses.

"After the service, feeling grand if a little foolish, we set off around the Green for the Russell Court Hotel, in our stately horse and carriage, drinking the complementary champagne, also laid on by the hotel. Sara was thrilled to be sitting up front with the driver.

"The meal lasted four hours, it was excellent but it took some time and effort for the thirteen adults to polish off the dozen bottles of champagne which arrived courtesy of my boss, Gerry Sinnott.

"We stayed the night at the Russell Court. Sara went home with granny and the rest repaired to the nightclub.

"Believe it or not the most memorable part of the day was the story of how our Mini was brought to the hotel.

"When we were setting off in the horse and carriage Stephen gave my brother the keys and told him where we had parked our car. When my brother got into the Mini he was surprised to find the seat so far forward, Stephen is 6 foot 3. He was driving around the Green when he noticed a baby seat in the back which set him wondering. When he got to the hotel the Mini caused great consternation. It wasn't ours. Giving him the number of our car, we sent him off to put the car he had back in its spot before he was arrested and to collect our car.

"By the time he got back, the place where the car had been parked was gone and the nearest spot he could find was around the corner. So there's somebody out there, who knows that they parked their car off Molesworth Street on a Friday in 1988 only to find it had moved when they got it back. It must have caused some head scratching. Our car was duly collected and brought to the Russell Court Hotel. That was our day, it was great. Since then we have been joined by Amy who is four and three year old Oscar."

ANN AND LUKE HAYDEN

Whether you can get married on a Sunday in your local church varies, for a variety of reasons, from county to county. With their hectic Sabbath duties, many priests and ministers feel under enough pressure and frankly, don't want any extra duties, thank you very much.

Check with your local priest or minister is the advice given, different parishes operate under different rules.

In Meath and Kildare it is possible to marry on Sunday, especially in quiet parishes.

In Dublin, Sunday weddings are out because the clergy are already under such pressure just catering for the pastoral needs of the capitals ever increasing population. But where there is an urgent need it can be catered for with the cooperation of the parish priest or bishop.

Around the country, Sunday weddings are out mainly because of Sunday funerals.

If however, you are Dublin-based and for some reason, desire to get married on a Sunday, like Ann and Luke Hayden, you may find where there's a will there's a way, and that way may be just a few miles beyond the Dublin border.

Ann is a theatrical agent and MD of Ann Curtis Agency, 59 Waterloo Road, Dublin 4, Ph 6602113. She met Luke in 1991, when he returned to Dublin from London and was advised by a friend to register himself on her books.

"The first time we met I told Luke he'd have to make an appointment to see me. Having lived in London for twelve years he was very much a bachelor and my firm policy was never to date clients, you don't mix business with pleasure etc.

"Soon after Luke registered, I took him to a casting director and somewhere between my office and the casting director's office my no dating the client policy went missing.

"We lived together for two years without either of us giving any thought to marriage. On Easter Saturday night 1993 our two-month-old daughter, Saoirse, was christened in Haddington Road and next morning Luke proposed.

"Being absolutely broke we planned a small family wedding for Friday 27th August. Small in my case is very much a relative term. I am the youngest in a family of ten, I have forty nieces and nephews. Luke's family is confined to his mother and sister. I booked Haddington Road Church and the Kingston Hotel in Dun Laoghaire, for sixty-five people with an extra 150—200 to arrive that evening.

"We thought the Kingston was brilliant. It's in a very romantic setting, overlooking Dun Laoghaire Harbour and Howth. We began to make the usual plans.

"Luke was in the play, *All My Sons*, at the Focus which was due to end its run in early August. You could say everything was set fair to sail.

"But then the play, which had got rave reviews, was invited to extend its run into the Theatre Festival and now, suddenly, Luke was very much unavailable to get married on Friday. While being delighted that the play had done so well, I wanted to cry with disappointment at having to cancel the wedding.

"Then Luke decided we'd get married on the Sunday instead.

"I rang the hotel who moved mountains to accommodate us. Then I contacted the priest in Haddington Road who said no way, it wasn't allowed in Dublin by the Archbishop. I don't know why, but I decided this was a job for Fr Cleary. I believed if he couldn't help us, no one could. Neither of us knew Fr Cleary, but I know an engineer with 98 FM.

Marry with Taste

"I rang him to ask him to ask Fr Cleary if I could come in and talk to him. Fr Cleary immediately agreed to see me. When I went in, he said, OK Ann, tell me your story, and don't worry, God'll work something out. Boy, was he a dynamo.

"Next day, Friday, he collected myself, Luke and Saoirse in his car and drove us out to look at two churches in Co Meath.

"The first church was in Kilbride and when he told us it was the church RTE used to film *The Riordans,* in we thought it was apt as well as being beautiful. As it happens, Fr Cleary's sister is sacristan there. We didn't go to see the second church, we absolutely fell for Kilbride. Within hours Fr Cleary had arranged to marry us there at one o'clock on Sunday, 29th August.

"On the day Fr Cleary was absolutely brilliant. Our wedding ceremony was magnificent. Fr Cleary was in great form, despite the fact that directly after our wedding, he drove himself to hospital to start treatment for throat cancer. He was absolutely amazing. He made our day. Ann Kent, an actress, was in *Widow's Peak* at the time with Mia Farrow. She arranged the car as a wedding present. It was an Al Capone-type vintage car used for the film. A young designer, just out of college, made my dress for £150. It would have cost £1,000 in the shops. I designed it around a dress I'd seen on Grace Kelly in a movie. It was a sleeky satin and lace number with a very long lace train, bustier top, and an old-fashioned halter strap around the neck. I wanted a tiara but couldn't get one anywhere because they were all sold out from the May communions. When my sister heard about my problem she gave the tiara which my my niece had used for her Holy Communion so that solved that problem. I had five bridesmaids and Luke had a best man and four groomsmen. Luke wore a John Rocha, A-Man suit. The vocalists, clients of mine, sang at our wedding as a wedding present. The soprano, Ann Buckley, had just won an opera award and Morgan Crowley, the baritone, had just been invited to join an American quartet. The two of them were in top form and sang spine-tingling solos and duets that made the walls shake.

"Our best man, Hubert Carbery, made our cake. Neil Frazer from the *Star* came straight from a shoot with Naomi Campbell to do the photographs, and Luke's sister's boyfriend from London did the video.

"Saoirse was at the church, a rosebud, in pink and white. We didn't want a sedate sit-down meal. We had a cold buffet and one hot dish, Chicken à la Kingston, the food was absolutely delicious, everyone could pick what they wanted. We had a disco afterwards.

"We spent our wedding night in the Westbury Hotel, who threw in the Bridal Suite at no extra charge. The following weekend we were invited back to the Kingston Hotel for a champagne candle-lit dinner and breakfast in bed next morning.

"Our honeymoon was short but very stylish. Yes, we had a most beautiful wedding day, all thanks to the intervention of Fr Michael Cleary."

GARY AND FRANCES BUCHANAN

Of all the weddings I have heard about in the course of researching this book, none brought the tears to my eyes as readily as this miracle wedding in Medjugorje. Miracle in the sense that it was magic.

In fact, I shouldn't really mention this wedding at all, because it goes against the whole purpose of this book, the need to plan. I use it because it is the exception that proves the rule.

Frances Buchanan believes and has much evidence to show, that if you put God first, everything else falls into place. She has great devotion to Our Lady too and firmly believes that it was due to the mother of God that she and her husband, Gary, had such an unforgettable wedding day. Gary, you sense, is less convinced than his wife about exactly why the day went so well, but he does agree, their cup overflowed on that day.

It happened like this. In January 1991, Frances was booked on a group pilgrimage to Medjugorje, led by the Catholic priest, Fr Aidan Carroll. The war in Yugoslavia was in progress, plane flights were uncertain, but the troubles had not yet reached Medjugorje.

"Myself and Gary planned to marry some day but we had no money and getting married in Ireland is an expensive exercise and we didn't even fancy the idea anyway. So, absolutely joking, I turned to Gary and said, "Why don't you come to Medjugorje with me, you know, we could get married there." He said, "Why not?" We hadn't a clue what we needed. To speed things up I went to and fro with documents ending up in the Archbishop's house to get the Nulla Osta form. I went to the Department of Foreign Affairs but found them hopelessly uninformed. They had no information and what they had was utterly confusing.

"I eventually sorted things out for myself, the hard way. I rang the Yugoslavian embassy in London and was informed that to marry in Yugoslavia we'd have to stay for ninety days, and hire an interpreter. The Yugoslavians were of the opinion that we'd have to get married civilly first, before we left Ireland and then marry in a religious ceremony in Medjugorje. The Department of Foreign Affairs concurred with that opinion."

Gary takes up the story. "I went into the Registry Office to arrange for our civil wedding for May 24th, the day before we were due to leave Ireland. I brought money with me and offered to pay in advance but was told not to bother paying until the day of the marriage.

"I was told to either put a notice in the papers or have the banns read out in church. We had the banns read out in church."

Because Gary has forgotten the finer details, Frances takes up the story again while breast-feeding their third child and third son Jake.

"On Friday 24th May, as arranged, we got ourselves sort of dressed up and barrelled into the Registry Office with our two witnesses, Helen and Ray O'Gorman and Gary's mother.

"The lady in the Registry Office told us that because Gary had not paid a deposit no wedding had been booked and nothing could be done. Gary nearly blew a gasket, his mother started to cry, I got onto our priest in Portmarnock, Fr Barry Murphy, who pleaded with them, but no. At this stage, I was of the impression that if I was not married civilly I could not be married in Medjugorje and my heart was broken.

"Then I remembered Fr Aidan Carroll, the pilgrimage leader, has rooms in St Stephen's Green. We took off like a shot; myself, Gary's mother, Ray and Helen. We charged through the Green in a single line, we must have looked like mad extras off a film set.

"Fr Aidan Carroll is a sea of tranquility. When I told him of our problems he said, 'Don't worry, the Lord will provide.' He assured us we didn't have to be married civilly first.

"Outside arranging the documents, the only plan we made specially for our wedding was my dress. My aunt, Angela O'Reilly, made me a ballerina length, cream satin and lace dress, and cream silk flowers for my hair. It was very simple but beautiful. Gary brought his best grey suit and grey tie. Next day, Saturday May 25th, we flew to Medjugorje, at 5.30 p.m.

"We didn't actually tell anybody about getting married but the whole plane knew it before we landed.

"When our group discovered that we were on our own with no family they asked us to let them be our family at the wedding. We said yes. A member of the group, Noel Hobbs (who, it turned out, knew Gary's mother well), asked us if he could give me away because, not having a daughter, only sons, he'd never had the chance to walk up the aisle and he'd always wanted to. I said yes, I'd be delighted. When Maureen Brennan, another member of the group, heard that my parents were dead she said she would act as the mother of the bride. So now I had a mammy and daddy.

"On Sunday morning, Fr Aidan Carroll met Fr Slavco to find out when and where we would be allowed to marry. They're not used to foreign weddings at Medjugorje so there is no set formula. The wedding was arranged for the next day, Monday at 12.00, at the Chapel of Adoration.

"On Monday morning at 6 a.m., the rain was pelting. I had breakfast and went off to see the visionary, Visca. I got back at 11 a.m., with my hair wet and started to prepare for the wedding at twelve.

"In the guest house where we were staying Rosario Hayeshcoy, a woman from the Portuguese embassy in Ireland, was ironing. When she heard that I had no flowers she rushed off to the florist and with mime and body language, she got across the message that she wanted flowers to make up a bouquet. When the florist twigged that the flowers were for a wedding he insisted she take the flowers as a present. They were absolutely beautiful. I was five minutes late arriving at the church and Gary was there biting his nails.

"Before I went into the church, Sheila Tighe from Blackrock, asked me if she could do me the honour of videoing the wedding. I said certainly.

"I had already arranged for two people from our group, James Murphy and Beth Fitzpatrick to be best man and bridesmaid.

"When I walked into the church on Noel's arm I was absolutely astonished. I expected to see our small group, instead, the church was packed with rows of Germans, Americans and Japanese. They cried through the entire ceremony. It was beautiful, simple, natural, meaningful, so moving. Fr Aidan's charisma is legendary. He is great at chanting and leading hymns and people just follow him. The feeling of God's love for everyone sent a glow through us all.

"I'll never forget the seventeen stone, 6 foot 4 German, whose face was covered in floods of tears as we walked down the aisle. Afterwards, they all came over and thanked us saying they were never at an 'Irish wedding' before.

"Outside the church, we met the American priest, Fr Rooky, whose special gifts have been extensively documented in America. That was a special moment. He blessed not only us, but our children and our children's children. Inside the church, Fr Aidan got everyone in the church to sign a form which he presented to us afterwards on a sort of parchment. It's a treasured document.

Marry with Taste

"During the wedding service, I knelt on a cream lace cushion. I didn't know that a woman from Dublin had made this cushion specially, before she left Ireland, when she heard about the wedding through Fr Aidan. She presented it to us, our first wedding present, after the wedding. I couldn't get over the amount of love and goodwill we experienced.

"We signed the register in the company of Fr Slavco who deals directly with the visionaries. He is a lovely humble and friendly priest and it means a lot to me that our wedding is registered in the Parish of St James, that's the main church in Medjugorje.

"We went to a café for coffee and when they heard we were the wedding party, they added alcohol to the coffee and said 'No Pay.' These are all very poor people and we were really astonished at their generosity.

"When we got back to the house we were going up to change for the four o'clock meal, but Fr Aidan asked us to stay dressed. I should have suspected something, but I really didn't. This is a very poor country and dinner is usually a fairly frugal affair with five long tables seating eight at each table.

"We went upstairs to freshen up and when we came down there was a huge cake, chocolate with fondant icing of cream flowers and FRONCES AND GORRY in a heart in the centre. The pink champagne was flowing and everyone was clapping. I was so overcome by the occasion I could hardly fight back the tears and Gary who is never lost for words was the same. We had gone to Medjugorje for what we thought would be a quiet simple wedding, what we got was more like the Feast of Cana, the love in the room was tangible.

"After dinner we had a singsong, and then at 6.40 p.m. when the visionary appears, Fr Aidan called for hush. Many of the people in our group had the gift of tongues and they started to pray to Our Lady.

"When the prayers were over we got into our

mountain climbing gear and went to the Podbro Mountain. We started the climb at 7.30 p.m., got there at 9.00 p.m., had prayers and came back down. For the rest of the week we were greeted like celebrities, with strangers wishing us the best.

"A few days after we came back to Dublin we got married as arranged again, in the Registry Office. We didn't bother to get especially dressed up, we looked on it as a mere formality. Helen and Ray brought their kids, we brought our five-year-old son Dane, and afterwards we went for ice-cream. I don't know how anyone could get married in a Registry Office. It's so cold and unfeeling. I really feel we had a miraculous unforgettable wedding day in Medjugorje that has influenced our lives ever since."

The Second Marriage Or Remarriage

❦

Thomas Hardy was in the autumn of his life when he contracted his second marriage to his former secretary, Miss Dugdale. He was thwarted in his efforts to keep the marriage secret. The press got wind of the word, much to his annoyance. This excerpt is from a letter he wrote to his friend, Edmund Gosse, on 11th February 1914, eighty years ago:

"...long time friend and secretary, Miss Dugdale...in some unforseen way, the trifling incident had got into the London afternoon papers, so I was defeated in my intentions of telling you by letter. We thought it better to inform nobody beforehand, not even relations. You will understand all this."

Whatever about marrying in secret, never marry in haste. Helga Shenkov, a fifty-nine-year-old widow in Helsinki, will probably hold the hasty record for some time to come. For the freshly widowed Helga merely took time off to bury her second husband in Helsinki, at 11.00 a.m., before rushing home to prepare for her next marriage at 2.30 p.m. on the same day.

In fact, the National Association of Widows in Ireland advises people not to make any big changes to their lives for at least two years after the break-up of a marriage, regardless of whether the end was due to death or divorce.

Love may be sensational the second time around, but second marriages are fraught with many difficulties on the religious, social, psychological level and in Ireland there is an added layer of legal difficulties, where the absence of divorce has resulted in many clandestine, bigamous marriages, the parties to which are, not surprisingly, reluctant to speak.

In England, where divorce is allowed, statistics show that while first-time marriages are on the decrease, from 398,000 in 1981 to 355,000 in 1991, remarriages rose from 44,000 in 1981 to 48,000 in 1990.

Whether you read that as bad news for the first marriage or as good news for the second marriage probably depends on your religious convictions.

For Catholics the rule is a rigid one, unless the first marriage has been terminated by the death of either party, or an annulment has been granted, remarriage in a church is forbidden.

In the Church of Ireland, while remarriage is not forbidden, it is frowned upon, and what usually happens is the couple marry in the registry office and have their new arrangement blessed in a religious service that stops short of marriage. For the non-established churches, Quakers and Jews, remarriage is allowed.

For all of these reasons, second marriages tend to be low-key affairs, but that doesn't mean the occasion can't be celebrated to the full.

Should the Bride on her Second Marriage wear the Fairytale Regalia?

Opinion is divided. Originally, of course, the white gown symbolised virginity, which clearly it can't symbolise for the second marriage.

For many women, getting married is a legitimate excuse for them to fulfil their fantasy of being a Barbie doll for a day and the wedding day is the one legitimate day on which they can do that.

Weddings too numerous to remember never stopped Liz Taylor from wearing the white, indeed the wedding gowns in her wardrobe must out-number the dressing gowns.

Marry with Taste

Princess Anne chose a classic, simple cream ensemble by Tom Bowker for her recent second marriage. No doubt many will follow that lead. I hope they won't follow her choice of bouquet which was a decidedly dull all-green affair that looked like a bunch of heather in the photographs. And the floral decoration in her hair was apologetic too.

The moral of the story is, if you are going for something don't be faint-hearted, be impregnably certain of what you want and then carry it through.

Don't let the fact that the majority of women getting married for a second time wear a smart frock or sharp suit. If you want the full white whirl go for it. There are plenty of precedents, you won't be the first nor the last.

A forty-five-year-old widow, who married in white for the second time in 1992, told me that her bossy mother had insisted on buying her a white frothy creation for her first wedding. She hated it. This time around she choose her own gown, the style she had wanted twenty-five years ago. She was proud of the fact that she still took size 12, and even her mother admitted it was nicer.

In 1993, a sixty-something bought the full, long, white, beaded dress and train trousseau from Pronuptia, because, she explained, "I married in the austerity of the war years and want to do it properly this time."

Even the royals are divided on what is the politically correct wedding dress for the second-time bride.

Raine Spencer's third marriage to the French count, Jean François de Chambrun, on July 10th 1993, caused consternation when she arrived at the church in a volcanic pink and white printed silk taffeta with fitted bodice, fichu neckline and full skirt, designed by the French fashion designer, Ungaro, and estimated to have cost between £10,000 and £20,000. Whatever about taste, you'd have to admire her spunky spirit.

What's that Johnson said about the Second Marriage being a Case of Hope over Experience?

There is a body of research in America which shows that second marriages break up, not because of the incompatibility of the couple, but because of the interference of grown-up offspring and because of differences of opinion on the rearing of children which the couple find emotionally difficult to cope with and solve.

I talked to two couples, both of whom had experienced offspring difficulties, in one case resulting in the break-up of the marriage. Both wish to remain unidentified.

One couple are in their late thirties and their marriage reads like a fairytale but they didn't want publicity because of the hassle which his former spouse would make for their children.

The other couple married in their sixties; she had four grown-up, employed daughters, to his two, grown-up, employed sons.

Both enjoyed fulfilling careers.

Their courtship was a satisfactory affair that lasted for two years with the usual round of outings to the cinema and theatre. Both of them played golf and had holidayed together before they married. When they married, they decided to rent out her three-bedroomed semi, mainly because the property market was so slow. They intended selling it when things picked up. He sold his four-bedroomed house and they bought a fine six-bedroomed house, with enough space for all.

If space was not a problem, philosophic differences soon manifested themselves. To say the least, things didn't work out.

The three men quickly established that they expected the five women to do all of the housework, while the men obliged them by being out of the house playing golf!

Not surprisingly the women remonstrated and two years later they removed themselves, mother and all, back to the three-bedroomed semi.

He told me he now regretted that he hadn't been more understanding towards his new wife. He knows he let his sons' opinion influence him, when he should have stood firm and listened to her. He had not expected her to act so soon. Two years later he would still like her to come back.

She admits she listened to her daughters and is glad. She simply refuses all invitations to try again. You can't help wondering what might have happened if they had been home alone? Might things have worked out better? American researchers would say yes.

Remarriage after Divorce

In the absence of divorce in Ireland, the recognition of foreign divorces is a minefield that results in a complex and convoluted process when the divorced person seeks to remarry.

There are different procedures, depending on the country in which the divorce was granted. For instance, whether you were resident or domiciled in that country makes a crucial difference. To my mind, a person holding a foreign divorce and wishing to remarry should clarify the status of their divorce document with professional legal advice before approaching either a church or the civil register.

Remarriage after Annulment

If an annulment has been granted, regardless of the condition of the annulment (be that psychiatric, homosexual or lesbian or other grounds), the person wishing to remarry must contact the Marriage Tribunal which granted the annulment.

That person then signs a form, giving the Marriage

Tribunal permission to release the documentation of the annulment to the relevant church authority in order that the remarriage process can begin.

At no stage will the person who has been granted the annulment be allowed to see the evidence which resulted in his or her marriage being annulled. That remains church property for ever.

COUNTDOWN TO WEDDING DAY

Two Years Before:

Announce engagement...by papers/phone/bush fire.
Buy/insure ring.
Book church in writing.
Book hotel/marquee/local hall/pub in writing.

One Year Before:

Book photographer in writing.
Book video operator in writing.
Choose Bridesmaid/Bestman/Groomsman to ensure availability.

Six Months Before:

Contact church/registry office. Book time of wedding.
Book Catholic Pre-marriage course—DOMAS, 16 Nth Gt Georges St, Dublin 1.
Book florist in writing.
Book hotel for honeymoon night. If the wedding party are staying at the reception venue, ensure separate quarters. A Donegal GP and his new wife were given a room adjoining his parents on their wedding night!
Book wedding cake or make rich fruit cake.
Book honeymoon/Check passports for foreign honeymoon.
Meet dressmaker or shop for dress.
Book best man/groom/pageboy's outfits.
Draw up guest list.
Book transport for bridal party, unless hotel is

providing same.
Book guest bus.
Listen/choose/book music for church and reception venue.

Three Months Before:

Book wedding gift list with department store or make your own gift list.
Make or order wedding invitations.
Send out invitations/wedding list cards or do a ring around.
Book wedding icing of home-made cake.
Order personalised mass/service booklets.
Buy honeymoon outfit, lingerie, tights, gloves, mountain climbing boots, hairy socks!
Notify Registrar for registry office wedding.
Buy presents for bridesmaid/groomsman.

Two Months Before:

Compile a guest list of acceptances/regrets.
Set up stag and hen parties.
Start beauty programme.
Walk/swim or work out daily, thirty minutes a day will reap rewards. Increase fruit/veg/water intake.
Exclude or reduce fatty foods. See skin glow.
Learn deep breathing relaxation—it works wonders on the big day.

One Month Before:

Book hairdresser/manicurist/beautician.
Try different hairstyles with head-dress.
Buy cosmetics and favourite perfume.
Decide on table plan of guests.
Wear wedding shoes around house.
Hair cut and styled bride/groom.

Marry with Taste

One Week Before:

Dress rehearsal of clothes. If necessary, arrange alteration.
Organise the floral arrangement if you are the florist.
Speeches reduced to prompt words on pocket-size. index cards.
Church and readers rehearsal.
Best man takes charge of rings/service booklets/envelopes with church/register fees for payment before ceremony.
Seating plan for church with head usher if necessary.
Check travel time at the time of wedding.
Final phone call for car/cake/florist/video/photographer/musicians.
Pack suitcases for honeymoon with travel documents and passports.
Leave with appointed caretaker.
Appoint a trusted neighbour to guard house if the reception is or the presents are in the family home.

Night Before/Morning Wedding
Early Morning/Afternoon Wedding:

Pray. Chant mantra. Sing—it makes the brain function better.
Gentle swim or soothing bath—not too hot.
Banish stress and hypertension with deep breathing exercises.
Smile constantly; it exercises the facial muscles.
Appoint trusted relative to visit reception venue to check seating plan, flowers, cake and pre-wedding photo are in place.
Check bouquets are as ordered.
Visit hairdresser after swim or have hairdresser call to home.
Have reflexology/massage/aromatherapy session.

RELAX.
Take time with make up and beauty routine. RELAX.
Dress with help from bridesmaid. RELAX.
Put engagement ring on left hand. RELAX.
Have special word with mother. RELAX.
Head-dress/bouquet in place. Leave house with father.
GOOD LUCK.

NOTE ON THE AUTHOR

Dublin-born, Treasa Brogan has worked as a freelance journalist for most national newspapers and magazines, publishing feature articles, interviews, profiles and humorous pieces on a variety of topics. She writes a health column for *Woman's Way,* "It Happened To Me," and is a theatre critic for the *Evening Press.* She has broadcast on RTE, contributing to *Sunday Miscellany, The Arts Show* and various book programmes. She lives in Portmarnock with her husband, Patrick, and their three children, Claire, Conor and Ciarán.